What They Never Told You About Boston

(Or What They Did That Were Lies)

What They Never Told You About Boston

(Or What They Did That Were Lies)

By Walt Kelley

Down East Books
Camden, Maine

Down East Books
P.O. Box 679
Camden, Maine 04843

Contents

This book is dedicated to my wonderful wife,
Linda Morris Kelley, without whose love, dedication, and
incredible patience it would never have been written.

Additional Kudos

Special thanks to Pat Russell, an authority on Boston's history and a regular contributor to the *Boston Globe* and a regular columnist for the *Carriage News*. Upon review of the first manuscript, Pat sent the author back to the libraries for an additional three months of research. (Thank God!)

Also, to Tony Melton of the Boston Chapter of the American Red Cross, who, in a cab ride with the author, inspired the title of this book. Thanks, too, to Hugh O'Regan, of Town Taxi; Richard Johnson, Curator of the New England Museum of Sports; Sinclair Hitchings, Keeper of Prints at the Boston Public Library, and his associate, Aaron Schmidt.

And finally, my deepest apreciation to Philip Bergen, Librarian of The Bostonian Society. Philip gave the manuscript a most thorough edit, and his suggestions and comments now leave this non-historian totally comfortable with the completed product.

How This Book Came to Be

I WAS BORN in Boston. Lived there all my life. But it was not until I began driving a cab, about six years ago, that I suddenly discovered that I knew absolutely nothing about my own city. Visitors would get into my taxi and exclaim, "Oh, what a beautiful church! Driver, when was it built? Or, "Who is that statue of, over there in the mall?" Virtually everything that people came to Boston to see, to learn about, to experience and then take home with them to treasure, I had always taken for granted and had never explored. The damned tourists, it seemed, always asked the most embarrassing questions! In self-defense, I began to read everything I could get my hands on about my city. Over time, I taught myself the history of Boston. And I enjoyed sharing this newfound knowledge with both visitors and residents alike. I quickly discovered that most Bostonians were not unlike myself. It seems that we all visit the most exotic cities we can find, and return home a week later knowing more about those cities than their lifelong residents do. But we never get around to learning about the place where we live.

I also discovered that the most fascinating history about Boston is being lost and forgotten. It is well documented, all right, but it is buried in thick, dusty historical tomes that the average person would never read. I think that whoever said, "Histories were written by historians, for historians," was probably correct. I further discovered that some of the most important historic events that happened in Boston are being completely misunderstood by visitors and residents alike.

So, when one of my passengers said to me (after one of my mini-lectures about what really happened on the night of Paul Revere's famous midnight ride) that I should write a book and call it *What They Never Told You About Boston, or What They Did and Were Lies!*, I immediately knew that this was my book to write.

This little book, then, was written by a non-historian for non-historians, by a Bostonian for his fellow Bostonians and for all of you who enjoy our city. With love.

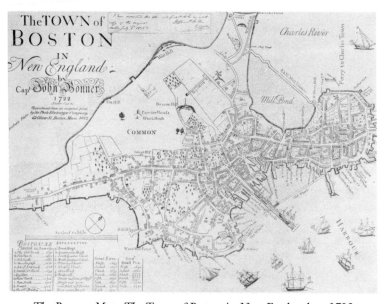

The Bonner Map: The Town of Boston in New England — 1722.
Courtesy of the Boston Public Library Print Department.

Introduction

And this is good old Boston,
The home of the bean and the cod,
Where the Lowells talk to the Cabots,
And the Cabots talk only to God.

—John Collins Bossidy, 1910

FOR CENTURIES visitors have been charmed by this quaint, pictur-
esque, historic little town with narrow, crooked streets and European
architecture. But no more so than Bostonians themselves who, since
1630, with what would become known as the Puritan ethic, worked
so very hard to create what has been called the Athens of America, the
Cradle of Liberty, the Hub of the Universe, the City on a Hill, and the
Mecca of Medicine. Bostonian pride has often been misconstrued as
haughty provincialism by some and as crass conservatism by others.
But a brief look at the record may suggest other roots.

From the beginning, Bostonians had to learn quickly to be re-
sourceful and self-sufficient. Fear of Indian attacks and starvation were
the two most important issues to address, and so the Puritans began
to teach their religious beliefs to the local Indians. Eventually, the
Puritan minister John Eliot even translated the first Bible into an
Indian language (Natick) and had it printed in Cambridge in 1661. As

the Indians were converted, they were no longer a threat, and they helped teach the settlers how to find and grow food.

In 1635 the first public school in America was established, Boston Latin School, followed one year later by Harvard College. Then Bostonians began not only to build the busiest seaport in the Western Hemisphere, ultimately trading across the globe, but also to "home-grow" physicians, theologians, philosophers, authors, artists, inventors, architects, business leaders, and philanthropists, as we shall later see.

No wonder, then, that Bostonians were loath to travel elsewhere when whatever they could possibly want was either already here or could be imported. One begins to understand why, in the late nineteenth century, when Maria Buckminster Moors Cabot read in the society page of a Boston newspaper that her good friend and sailing companion, Abigail Lowell, was taking her family on a trip to California, she exclaimed:

Oh, my God!
. . . And so far from the ocean!

Boston and its Environs —1775.
Courtesy of the Boston Public Library Print Department.

How We Got
Our Name

LET US START by going back to seventh-century England, to a little fishing village on the River Witham, in the district of Lincolnshire. In this little village lived a Benedictine monk who, by some accounts, was a bastard son of King Ethelmund. This monk would rise early each morning with the fishermen so that he could say a prayer for them and bless their boats before they went out to fish. As it was a general custom in early England to give people names based upon what they did, the fishermen named this monk Botulph—*bot*, in Old English, meaning boat and *ulph* meaning helper. Boat-helper. Of course, being a man of the cloth, he would help everyone in the village, but he did pay particularly close attention to the fishermen.

When this monk eventually died, the fishermen, their families, and the other villagers decided that, to properly honor his memory, they would rename their village after him. They named it Bot Ulph's Town. Botulph's Town. But they pronounced it Bottleston. And Bottleston, Bottleston, Bottleston, repeated rapidly and carelessly for decades, eventually was contracted into, and of course still is, Boston. Boston, England.

Now let us move forward in history, to 1630—September 7, to be precise. This is when John Winthrop and his Puritans, having left England to find religious freedom, arrived to settle in the New World. Virtually all of these first immigrants were from this very district of

Lincolnshire. This is why they ultimately named the town Boston, after their home village.

Eventually the seventh-century monk was canonized by the Church, and is today known as Saint Botolph, the patron saint of Boston. The first street was named in his honor in 1707, on Beacon Hill (renamed Irving Street in 1855). In 1880, the St. Botolph Club, one of Boston's famous literary clubs, was founded and St. Botolph Street in the Back Bay was named. (Curiously, the only St. Botolph's church in Boston is a small chapel housed within the YMCA on Huntington Avenue.)

Obvious and natural though the name Boston was, it was not the first English name given to this place! When Winthrop first arrived, what he discovered was a very narrow peninsula with virtually no land (approximately 783 acres). After short deliberation, he decided to try another side of the harbor, which had more land available and was more readily defensible. So he established a temporary settlement, which had been named "Charlestowne" by John Smith in 1624. From Charlestown, looking back across the water to what we know today as Beacon Hill, Winthrop then saw three hills. (Two have been completely leveled, and the third is now some sixty feet shorter than it was then—but more on this in Chapter 10.) Seeing these three hills, Winthrop gave us our first name, Trimountaine.

Charlestown, however, quickly proved unsuitable for a major settlement due to the lack of good drinking water. No matter how many wells were sunk, the water was always terribly brackish. So Winthrop went back to the little peninsula to see if the drinking water there were any better, and when he discovered that it was, he moved the major portion of his colony from Charlestown. And, since they had made the decision before leaving Lincolnshire, England, to name the first permanent settlement Boston, Winthrop soon changed its name from Trimountaine.

Later, one of the major streets of Boston was named Trimountaine. After the dictionary was invented, and names and places were no longer spelled and pronounced in numerous different ways, we were left with Tremont Street—where, in fact, Winthrop is buried at King's Chapel Burying Ground.

Indians actually lived on this little peninsula until several years prior to the arrival of the Puritans. It seems that the last resident tribe had been decimated by a plague, and henceforth most Indians considered it unsafe. Some would, however, use the peninsula seasonally to fish. These Native Americans, of course, had also named it: they called it Shawmut. Coincidently, both Boston and Shawmut have a common reference. Boston, as we have learned, comes from boat-helper. And *Shawmut*, loosely translated from the Wampanoag language, means "the place where you go to find boats"!

So, you see, they were wrong when they told you that Shawmut was the name of an Indian or the name of a tribe!

2

The First
Real Settler

IF, AFTER READING the previous chapter, you are convinced that you know who Boston's first English settlers were, you are due for a surprise. But you will not be as surprised as Winthrop was when he went back to sample the peninsula's drinking water.

When Winthrop made his first serious survey of the peninsula that he had earlier spurned, he found the westernmost part ended at what now is the Charles Street side of Boston Common. But, to his astonishment, he also discovered that an Englishman was already living close by, at what is now the western base of Beacon Hill.

The Reverend William Blaxton, an Anglican minister, had been living on the peninsula for over five years. He was one of the few survivors of the first attempt to settle Weymouth, Massachusetts, in 1623. Blaxton found his way some twenty miles north to this little peninsula with several bags of seeds and a substantial library. He built a wooden house, planted several acres of the peninsula, and had been living the life of a scholar-hermit when Winthrop found him. Today, a plaque at the corner of Beacon and Spruce streets marks the site of Blaxton's house.

Although not legally required to do so, as he had a charter from the King, Winthrop did the morally correct thing and offered to purchase the tiny peninsula in order to begin his permanent settlement. Blaxton agreed to a purchase price of thirty pounds sterling.

Fifty of the acres purchased from Blaxton were set aside "as a park for the feeding of cattle and for the militia to use as a training ground." Today, thanks to Winthrop's decision, the Boston Common remains the oldest public park in the entire country! Also, the oldest military organization in the country, the Ancient and Honorable Artillery Company, has used the Common at least annually for their training exercises since the company was formed, in 1638.

The Puritans left England in order to practice their religion without interference, but religious tolerance was not their own forte. Blaxton was an Anglican in a settlement of Puritans, and they desperately tried to convert him for well over a year. Blaxton foretold his future when he said, "I left England on account of the Bishops. . . . I fear that I may have to leave here on account of the Bretheren." Shortly thereafter, in 1632, he left for Rhode Island, where others dissenters such as Roger Williams, Anne Hutchinson, and many Quakers also fled or were banished. Once in Rhode Island, however, Blaxton shed his scholar-hermit habits and began to preach the theme of religious freedom. Because this again was a pre-dictionary era when names and places were frequently spelled and pronounced any number of ways, Blaxton became "Blackstone," and today several places in Rhode Island are named in his honor, including a river, some parks, and a valley, as well as a town just over the border in Massachusetts, where he once lived.

It took Bostonians two hundred years to honor the memory of the peninsula's first non-Indian resident. But eventually, in 1834, Blackstone Street (where the weekend pushcart market is in Dock Square) and Blackstone Square at Washington and West Newton streets in the South End were named in his honor.

The First Real Settler

3

The Beginning of Education

THE PURITANS FAILED to convert William Blaxton but succeeded in instilling many of the local Indians with the Christian faith. This freed Bostonians to address other important issues, such as education. So, in 1635, the first school in the colonies, Boston Latin School, was established.

For the school's first ten years, classes were held in the Master's house. Then, in 1645, the first schoolhouse was erected on the spot that is now the front of Old City Hall, across from the present Parker House Hotel. The street was then named Latin School Street, and, although the school was relocated several times beginning in 1688, it remained on this same street. The first move was to allow construction of King's Chapel, the first Anglican Church in the Colonies, and later the school yielded its space to the first Unitarian Church. It was not until after the school's fifth relocation, to Dartmouth and Warren streets in the South End, that its original street's name was shortened to its present name, School Street. Still the oldest public school in America, Boston Latin now is on Avenue Louis Pasteur, near Harvard Medical School and not far from Fenway Park.

Shortly after establishing a base at Boston, a small group of Puritans crossed the Charles River to acquire farmland, and there they established "Newtowne." In fact, so much land was available, compared to the tiny peninsula, that serious consideration was given to moving the seat of government from Boston to Newtowne.

At this same time, the Puritans recognized the need for an institution of higher learning in the commonwealth, especially for the training of clergy. A group of Bostonians approached the Great and General Court of the Commonwealth of Massachusetts with the following proposition: "Not only," they said, "should Newtowne be considered for the seat of government here in the Commonwealth, but also for the seat of all learning." You see, virtually all of the first Puritan leaders from Lincolnshire had graduated from Cambridge University, and to them Cambridge was "the seat of all learning." So Captain Robert Keayne, the leader of this particular group of Bostonians as well as founder of the Ancient and Honorable Artillery Company, argued that, "There should be established in Newtowne, the College at Cambridge." This argument, of course, did not fall upon deaf ears, as almost every member of the General Court was also a graduate of Cambridge. Thus in 1636, the General Court authorized the establishment of "The College at Cambridge in Newtowne."

Unfortunately, the government had not the means to fund the college. Although legally established, the college had no master, no buildings, and no students.

Then, in 1637, a stranger from England arrived and settled, with his wife, in Charlestown. Minister John Harvard happened to arrive at the apex of the Anne Hutchinson controversy, and he attended the Synod at Newtowne, which consisted of twenty-four days of theological discussion. Hutchinson took the antinomian view that faith alone is necessary for salvation. Her public avowal that the Gospels were irrelevant and that public acts did not prove inherent grace led to this synod. She was found guilty of "traducing the ministers," and for her heresy she was banished forever. It was at this synod that Harvard learned of the plan to establish the College at Cambridge. As historical coincidence so frequently has it, John Harvard was a Cambridge man himself!

Harvard's mother had been twice widowed, and on each occasion had been left a substantial inheritance. She died shortly before John left for the New World, and her estate was divided equally between her two sons. Shortly after Harvard arrived in the Massachusetts Bay Colony, his brother died, leaving John as sole heir. The brother's estate also included the Queenshead Inn—a tavern in Southwark, Surrey. John Harvard had become a wealthy young minister.

The Beginning of Education

When Harvard learned of this yet-to-start College at Cambridge, he mentioned to his wife that when he died he would like to bequeath the college half his estate, including the tavern in Surrey and his library of books. And then, believe it or not, he proceeded to die. On September 14, 1638, John Harvard died, and was later buried in the Old Phipps Cemetery in Charlestown, right in the shadow of the Bunker Hill Monument. His widow, extraordinarily by today's mores, informed authorities that, although her husband left no will, his wishes were that one half of his estate go to the College at Cambridge. When Captain Keayne and his associates discovered the generosity of this newcomer from England, they decided to honor this Harvard's memory by naming the college after him. The General Court quickly agreed, and also stipulated that Newtowne would henceforth be called Cambridge after "the seat of all learning."

Contrary to popular belief, then, John Harvard was not the founder of the college, just its first benefactor; technically, the General Court was the founder, though it could not finance the actual start-up. Even so, Harvard's statue in Harvard Yard has "Founder" inscribed on the base. This statue is by Daniel Chester French, one of America's best sculptors (creator of the Minuteman Statue, the Abraham Lincoln Memorial, and the bronze doors on the Boston Public Library, as well), but the inscription was not his, nor was the incorrect founding date of 1638. To French's great credit, upon discovering that Harvard had never been sketched, he actually searched out several of Harvard's collateral descendants, sketched them, and used a composite for the face on the statue. (Harvard and his wife had no children. And, although it was the custom for seniors at Cambridge University to sit for their portrait, for some reason, he never did so.)

Among other things they never tell you is that for its first several years, Harvard College was basically funded by the proceeds from the sale of alcohol at the Queenshead Inn. That was, until the tavern burned down in the 1640s, never to be rebuilt. To this day, wags say that the college still runs on alcohol.

Also, they conveniently forget to tell you this: when the school's first library, Harvard Hall, burned down in 1764, losing everything including the entire collection of John Harvard's books, an undergraduate appeared at the residence of the college president. The student had withdrawn a book, *The Christian Warfare,* by Downame,

Cover and title page of the only surviving book from
John Harvard's bequeath: The Christian Warfare.
Courtesy of Harvard College, Houghton Library.

from the library without permission. As a consequence, this was the only surviving book from John Harvard's bequest. The president joyously accepted the book and then permanently dismissed the student for having taken the book without permission!

What they do tell you, however, is that the motto at Harvard University is *Veritas,* which in Latin means Truth. But that is not what they spoke if they told you that Harvard was named for its founder.

4

Sumus Primi:
We Are First

SO MUCH HAS BEEN WRITTEN about Boston in the city's 360-plus years that, ironically, some of the most fascinating history lies buried deeply within serious historical tracts, all but forgotten. In the writer's many conversations with Bostonians (and visitors) who have an avid interest in the city, he has encountered their delight in discovering some of this almost-lost lore. One important and illustrative area is that in which Boston was the First.

The following is an attempt to catalogue most of these interesting and important firsts, but their number is so great that most will have to stand with little commentary.

1630	The first military training field was established by the settlers in Charlestown to prepare a defense against Indian attack.
1631	The first fire law was passed in the Colonies: No wooden chimneys were allowed.
1632	The first law against smoking in public was passed: "Nor shall any take tobacco in any inne, or common victual house, except in a private room there, so as the master of said house nor any guest there shall take offence, under pain of 2 shillings and sixpence for every such offence."

1634	Boston Common was set aside. This is both the first public park in America and the oldest public park in the world.
1635	Boston Latin School, the nation's first public school, was established. Its motto, *Sumus Primi*, means "We are first."
1636	Harvard College was legally established by the General Court. It was the first college in what later became the United States.
1636	The first recorded naval engagement took place in Boston Harbor: John Gallop found a bark (a small sailing vessel) belonging to his friend John Oldham full of Indians. He fought them successfully and recovered possession of the boat.
1637–8	The first women's religious discussion club in America was established by Anne Hutchinson, the leading spirit in the violent antinomian religious controversy.
1638	The first legal monopoly in this country occurred: the General Court granted Cambridge (more specifically, Harvard College) the exclusive right to operate printing presses.
1638	The Ancient and Honorable Artillery Company was established. Not only is it the oldest military organization in this country, but also it is the third oldest in the world.
1639	America's first post office was opened. The General Court authorized Richard Fairbanks's Tavern as the official repository of mail.
1640	The first book in America, the *Bay Psalm Book*, was printed in Cambridge, by Stephen Day.
1640	The first slaves in New England arrived by ship. The General Court immediastely ordered them returned. A few years later the court reversed itself and set no limit to the number of slaves a Bostonian could own so long as he had the means.
1641	The world's first statute against cruelty to animals was

adopted by the General Court: "It is ordered by this court that no man shall exercise any tyranny or cruelty towards any brute creatures which are usually kept for the use of man."

1644	The first bicameral legislature in America was established.
1647	The first compulsory school law was enacted, calling for "a teacher for every community of 50 families or more."
1648	Shoemakers and coopers formed the first North American guild. They were authorized by the court to elect their own officers and clerks for the first time. Previously, the officers were appointed by the court.
1648	Salem suffers the infamy, but "witches" were first hanged in Boston: Margaret Jones was the first, and three others were hanged in Boston after her.
1649	The first water works: a twelve-foot-square reservoir covered with planks was built at Union and North streets, and piped to supply fresh water for fighting fires.
1650	America's first poem was published (in London). It was Bostonian Ann Bradstreet's "The Tenth Muse Lately Sprung Up in America."
1652	America's first coins, the Pine Tree Shillings, were minted in Boston by John Hull.
1656	The first environmental law was enacted: The only place that butchers might "throw their beasts' entrails and garbid, without penalty of a fine, is from the bridge to the North End." (If they told you that the pollution of Boston Harbor began at the time of the Industrial Revolution, they lied to you!)
1661	The first Bible printed in an Indian language (Natick) was published in Cambridge, translated by Puritan minister John Eliot.
1662	The first major bridge was built. A wooden drawbridge known as the Great Bridge was constructed on the site of the present Larz Anderson Bridge and connected

Boston to Cambridge and Harvard College.

1662	America's first official censor was appointed. Boston continued to have an official censor until 1975. (A film, play, or book "Banned in Boston" could make millions for authors, especially from the 1920s to the 1970s.)
1673	A fencing school, the first in the Colonies, was established in Boston.
1679	The first building code was enacted: After the great fire of 1679, houses and warehouses had to be constructed of brick or plastered on the outside with a strong cement mixed with gravel and glass, and roofed with slate.
1683	The first fire "engine" in America, in Boston's North End, was described on a broadside (a poster).
1686	The first commercial bank in the Colonies was established in Boston.
1690	The first newspaper in America, *Publick Occurrences, Both Foreign and Domestick,* was published. It was immediately banned.
1694	The first public drinking law was passed: All taverns had to post a list of common tipplers, and a proprietor caught serving any of them was subject to a fine or closing.
1698	The first road map for public use was published: "The Map of New England."
1700	The first anti-slavery tract in the Colonies was published by Samuel Sewall.
1704	The *Boston News-Letter*, America's first regular newspaper, was published, as was the first newspaper advertisement (offering to sell a mill at Oyster Bay, New York).
1704	The first travelogue: Madame Knight's trip from Boston to New York was publicly recounted.
1716	The Boston Light, America's first lighthouse, was built.

1721	Dr. Zabdiel Boylston introduced smallpox inoculation to Boston.
1722	The first billiards parlor opened, in Charlestown.
1724	America's first insurance office, the Sun Fire Office of Boston, opened at what is now 22 State Street.
1728	The first paper mill in America, in Dorchester Lower Mills, began operations.
1729	The first math textbook was published. It was titled *Arithmetick, Vulgar and Decimal.*
1731	The first public concert in America was held.
1733	America's first Grand Lodge of Masons was established at the Bunch of Grapes Tavern on King Street (now State Street).
1744	The first music society, the Stoughton Music Society, was founded by a group of Harvard men.
1744	The first set of bells was brought to North America to be installed in the Old North Church.
1765	The first chocolate factory, which later became Walter Baker Chocolate, was built.
1779	America's first Academy of Arts and Sciences founded.
1782	The country's first medical school, Harvard Medical School, was established.
1785	The first American bridge across a broad, deep river was built to Charlestown from Boston's North End. (It was longer than the Tower Bridge in London.)
1790	The first independence monument in America was erected on the summit of Beacon Hill. It was designed by Charles Bulfinch.
1790	The first American ship to circumnavigate the globe (the *Columbia*) began her journey from Boston.
1791	The nation's oldest historical society, The Massachusetts Historical Society, was founded.
1795	America's first "labor union" was organized by Paul

Revere. It was open to several trades.

1799	The first Board of Health was formed.
1803	The first "gravity" railroad was built to level Mount Vernon, one of the three original hills now singly called Beacon Hill.
1808	America's first hotel, the Exchange Coffee House, was opened. It was destroyed by fire in 1818.
1815	The first Sunday School services in America were held at Christ Church (the Old North Church).
1815	The Handel and Haydn Society, the oldest continuously performing group in the United States, performed *The Messiah* for the first time in America.
1820	America's first Mercantile Library was opened.
1826	The first horse-drawn railway was spawned by construction of the Bunker Hill Monument, to move Quincy granite to the docks at Neponset, where it was transported by boat to Charlestown.
1827	The first horticultural society in the United States, the Massachusetts Horticultural Society, was established.
1827	America's first swimming school was established.
1832	The first public school system was established by Horace Mann. Convinced that education was the means by which the individual creates for himself a full personal life, Mann went to Europe and studied many foreign school systems. He modeled the Massachussets system after the German schools that placed students in class grades according to age.
1832	"America," written by Bostonian Samuel Francis Smith in 1831, was first sung at Park Street Church.
1833	Dr. Samuel Gridley Howe, husband of Julia Ward Howe, founded the first community service for the blind. It was later renamed the Perkins School for the Blind after a gift of property from Thomas H. Perkins.

1834	Ice was first shipped to India from Boston. Tightly packed with sawdust in the holds of ships, over eighty percent of the ice survived the voyage. Several Boston family fortunes were made shipping ice.
1834	The first homeowners association, the Louisburg Square Proprietors' Association, was formed.
1837	The first passenger elevator in the United States was installed in the Crawford House in Scollay Square.
1842	America's first "spring floor" for a dance studio was installed. With springs under the hardwood, the floor was easier on the dancers' feet and knees.
1843	Dr. Samuel Gridley Howe for the first time in educational history trained a deaf, mute, and blind person at Dr. Howe's institute for the blind. The student was Laura Bridgeman.
1845	The New England Historical Genealogical Society, the first of its kind in the United States, was formed.
1846	The first use of ether during surgery was at Massachusetts General Hospital by Dr. W.T.G. Morton, a dentist.
1851	The first Y.M.C.A. in America was founded.
1851	The first electric fire-alarm system was constructed by Dr. William P. Channing and Moses Gerrish.
1851	The Union Boat Club, the oldest rowing club in America, was established.
1857	The first school band was formed at the Boston Asylum and Farm School for Indigent Boys, located on Thompson's Island. (In 1956, the institution became Thompson Academy, a private four-year school.)
1857	The first apartment house in America, the so-called French Flats, was built at Tremont and Boylston streets by Dr. John H. Dix. It was named the Hotel Pelham.
1858	The first burglar alarm system in America was installed by Edwin T. Holmes.

1859	Land was set aside for the first Public Garden in the United States.
1860	The first aerial photograph shot in America was taken: Boston from a balloon on October 13, by James W. Black.
1861	The first kindergarten was founded by Elizabeth Palmer Peabody.
1861	Julia Ward Howe wrote "The Battle Hymn of the Republic."

The first aerial photograph taken in the United States was this "Balloon View of Boston," dated October 13, 1860.
Courtesy of the Boston Public Library Print Department.

Massachusetts Institute of Technology:
Rodgers Building, School of Architecture, in
Copley Square. Photo c. 1870.
Courtesy of the Boston Public Library Print Department.

1862	The first football game in America was played on the Boston Common.
1863	The first all-Black regiment, the Massachusetts 54th, went to war.
1865	The Massachusetts Institute of Technology opened at Copley Square. Shortly thereafter, M.I.T. established America's first school of architecture.
1865	The first public bath house in America, the L Street Bath House, was opened.
1865	The first U.S. statue cut from granite was created by William Rimmer. It is the statue of Alexander Hamilton located on the Commonwealth Avenue Mall.
1866	The first Y.W.C.A. in the United States was established. Thirty women gathered at the home of Mrs. Henry F. Durant and founded the Boston Y.W.C.A. They soon

opened two houses on Beach Street for young women who came from rural areas to work in the city. Opposed by citizens who thought women should not live independently, Mrs. Durant explained: "There will always be young women dependent upon their own exertions for support."

1867 This country's oldest music conservatory, The New England Conservatory of Music, was founded in Boston.

1869 The first statue ever erected of a mounted George Washington, created by Thomas Ball, was placed in the Public Garden.

1871 The first branch library in the United States opened at the former Lyman School in East Boston.

1871 The first double-decked stadium in America was built at Walpole Street (called the South End Grounds) and was

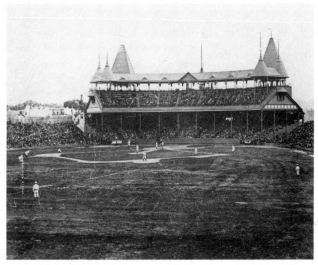

The first double-decked grandstands in America. South End Grounds at Walpole Street in 1871. It was the home field for Boston's National League Baseball Club.
Courtesy of The Bostonian Society.

used by the National League Baseball Club, later named the Boston Braves.

1872 — Bostonian Julia Ward Howe first proposed a Mother's Day for the United States and held annual meetings of mothers in Boston thereafter.

1872 — The first trained nurse in America was graduated from the country's first training school for nurses: the New England Hospital for Women and Children, in Boston. Her name was Linda Richards.

1875 — The first Christmas card in America was printed by Louis Prang. He created an ornate, flowery card with a colorful Christmas scene (and no preprinted message).

1875 — Alexander Graham Bell invented the electric speaking telephone.

1877 — America's first telephone exchange, complete with operators, was set up. It served Boston and Cambridge.

1877 — Robert Paget invented the swan boats. The Paget family still operates the swan boat concession in the Public Garden.

1878 — America's first bicycle factory and bicycle club were established. Also, the first bicycle race in the United States was held, won by C.A. Parker of Harvard. (He completed the three-mile course in twelve minutes, twenty-seven seconds.)

1879 — The First Church of Christ Scientist was chartered by Mary Baker Eddy.

1879 — The oldest art association now in America, The Copley Society, began.

1879 — The Archaeological Institute of America was organized in Boston with Charles Eliot Norton as its first president.

1880 — Beethoven's First and Fifth symphonies were first performed in the United States, by the Boston Academy for Music.

*The first public building with electric lights was the Hotel
Vendôme, on the right in this view from the 1880s. Outdoor
lights may be seen in front of the top dormer window.*
Courtesy of the Boston Public Library Print Department.

1882	The Hotel Vendôme, at Commonwealth Avenue and Dartmouth Street, became the first commercial building in America to have electric lights.
1884	The nation's first public park *system*, Frederick Law Olmsted's "Emerald Necklace" was begun.
1885	The first Irish-American mayor of a major U.S. city, Hugh O'Brien, was elected.
1892	The Pledge of Allegiance was written by Francis Bellamy, at 142 Berkeley Street, since named the "Pledge of Allegiance Building."
1893	Harvard Divinity student Arthur Shurtleff began the tradition of a lighted candle in the window at Christmas time at his parents' home on West Cedar Street.

1896	*The Boston Cooking School Cook Book*, by Fanny Farmer, became the first cookbook published in our country. Also, the Boston Cooking School, the first cooking school in America, was started by Fannie Farmer that same year.
1897	America's first streetcar subway was opened. It ran from Park Street to the Arlington Street station.
1897	The first Boston Marathon was run with only sixteen contestants. Today, almost ten thousand run in this, America's oldest marathon.
1899	The first Animal Rescue League was established.
1902	Architect Ralph Adams Cram started the tradition of Christmas caroling outdoors (on Beacon Hill).
1903	Harvard Stadium, the first football stadium, was opened.
1903	The first World Series game was played at the Old Huntington Avenue Baseball Grounds. (Cy Young, pitching for the Boston team, lost.)
1913	The nation's first credit union was opened by the

The site of the first drawbridge in America, and Harvard Stadium, the oldest outdoor stadium in the United States.
Courtesy of The Bostonian Society.

Women's Educational and Industrial Union.

1916 | The Union Bookshop published *The Horn Book*. This was the first publication to evaluate children's literature.

1919 | Boston Police formed a union and conducted the first "strike against public safety," in the words of Governor Calvin Coolidge.

1924 | The first American hockey team to enter the National Hockey League was the Boston Bruins in the 1924–25 season.

1928 | The first computer, "the differential analyzer," was developed at M.I.T.

1936 | The first federally funded public housing project in the United States was started in South Boston: the Mary Ellen McCormack Project.

1940 | The first chartered mutual life insurance company in the United States, the New England Mutual Life Insurance Company, opened in Boston.

1941 | The first and now the largest public sailing program in America began. It is simply called Community Boating.

1942 | The first modern fire codes were enacted as a result of the Coconut Grove fire, which killed 491 persons.

1944 | The first automatic digital computer was developed at Harvard.

1950 | The first Black basketball player, Chuck Cooper of Duquesne University, was drafted into the National Basketball Association by the Boston Celtics.

1957 | The first Black professional hockey player in the National Hockey League was Willie O'Ree of the Boston Bruins.

1966 | The first Black head coach in professional sports was Bill Russell with the Boston Celtics.

Quite a list of firsts for America, and all from Boston!

Sumus Primi: *We Are First*

5

Skeletons in the Closet

BOSTON'S HISTORY contains an ongoing litany of injustices to many individuals and groups, starting with the early repression by the Puritans, continuing to the recent past with the conservative influence of the Roman Catholic Church. (For several decades, ending in the mid-1970s, in fact, the population of the city of Boston was more than fifty percent Catholic.) Ironically, Boston's history is also replete with some of the most progressive and liberal legislation passed in this country. But to properly understand and appreciate Boston, some skeletons must come out of the closet.

The Puritan influence is seen immediately as we find that in 1631, only Puritan Church members (male) had the right to vote. The intolerance suggested by such a law has continued unabated until only very recently, and is remarkable not only for its longevity but also for its vigor. For example, it was not until 1966 that the law banning all forms of contraception was finally repealed. Also, the city had an official censor until 1975. Many of the laws passed by the General Court in the seventeenth century are still "on the books" in the Commonwealth of Massachusetts. They have always been referred to by Bostonians as the Blue Laws.

Now for our last long list of things that they not only did not tell you about Boston, but also hoped that you never found out.

1631	For impiety, Philip Ratcliff had both his ears cut off.
1635	A persecuted Roger Williams fled to Rhode Island.
1637	Anne Hutchinson was banished for "traducing the ministers."
1637	The local Pequot Indian tribe was wiped out by the settlers.
1643	Two lovers were hanged for adultery.
1644	All Baptists were banished from Massachusetts.
1644	The General Court ordered that all Indians must worship God.
1646	Presbyterians were banished from Massachusetts.
1648	The first of four "witches," Margaret Jones, was hanged in Boston.
1651	Fancy dress and dancing were forbidden.
1655	Irish immigrants arrived in Boston and were sold into bondage.
1656	"Witch" Ann Hibbens died on the gallows at Boston Neck, a narrow causeway leading from Boston to Roxbury.
1656	Quakers were banished under penalty of death.
1660	Mary Dyer was the last of four Quakers hanged in Boston.
1662	Official censors were appointed.
1670	Ten thousand rogues, vagabonds, and beggars were shipped from England, and some were sold as slaves in the Colonies, many in Boston.
1673	The Massachusetts General Court decreed that all church doors must be locked during services to keep the members from leaving!
1675–6	Forty Indians captured in King Philip's War were executed on Boston Common.

Skeletons in the Closet

1688	Mrs. Glover, a "witch" from Ireland, was hanged on the Boston Neck.
1700	Catholic priests were banned in and about Boston.
1721	The Reverend Cotton Mather's house was firebombed for his support of Dr. Zabdiel Boylston's attempt to introduce smallpox inoculation.
1723	Benjamin Franklin fled from Boston to Philadelphia to escape the cruelty and tyranny of his brother.
1724	A bounty was offered by town officials for the scalp of a Jesuit priest, Father Rasle.
1726	Hoop petticoats were condemned in Boston as being against God's law.
1750	All stage performances were officially banned in Boston. This law was not repealed until 1797.
1765	The first annual anti-Catholic "Pope's Day" celebration was heavily attended. (The Catholic Mass was not said in public in Boston until 1788.)
1834	The Ursuline Convent (Catholic) in Charlestown was burned down by bigots.
1835	Abolitionist William Lloyd Garrison was mauled by a Boston mob.
1849	Racial segregation of Boston schools was ruled legal by the courts.
1855	Several Boston police were fired on grounds of nationality. They were Irish.
1914	Censorship was again carried out in earnest. Included among the many plays banned in Boston were: Edward Albee's *Who's Afraid of Virginia Woolf?*, Sean O'Casey's *Within the Gates*, and Eugene O'Neill's *Strange Interlude*. Many books, such as William S. Burroughs' *Naked Lunch* and D.H. Lawrence's *Lady Chatterley's Lover*, were also banned. When the official censor, Richard Sinnott, closed the production of *Hair* in Boston, and

the Court ordered it reopened four weeks later, it was the end of all official censorship. That year was 1970!

1945	The Massachusetts Legislature finally revoked the Edict of Banishment against Anne Hutchinson.
1966	The law that banned all forms of contraception was finally repealed.

In addition to the sorry truths above, there are many other little-known facts in Boston's history—the realities of some other very important historical events, which, over the centuries, have been exaggerated to the point where, in our public consciousness, we have them greatly askew.

6

The Boston Massacre

ONE MISUNDERSTOOD historical event is the Boston Massacre of 1770. First, some background: we should remember that the fury of Bostonians began in 1765, with the Stamp Act, which was imposed as a revenue source for England. As a result, the Sons of Liberty formed, and their protests did not take the form of simple "civil disobedience." Royal Governor Thomas Hutchinson's house was all but destroyed and everything in it was destroyed or stolen by anti–Stamp Act mobs. With violent protests taking place regularly, Parliament nevertheless enacted, in 1767, the Townshend Act, which taxed imports to the Colonies on, among other things, tea. As a result, most Boston merchants refused to import British goods, and smuggling proliferated. Immediately, British Customs collectors were sent to Boston; in 1768, when they seized John Hancock's ship *Liberty* for smuggling, the customs collectors were set upon and badly beaten by a Boston mob. So King George III sent regiments of his redcoats to Boston to impose law and order.

The occupation of the city gave Bostonians large numbers of visible stand-ins for the "tyrant George" upon whom they could vent their rage. And their expression of outrage was not limited to the ever-increasing number of meetings held by the Sons of Liberty in taverns and under the Liberty tree, nor to the public meetings in Faneuil Hall, usually chaired by Sam Adams. Verbal and physical confrontations with the redcoats abounded. Heads were bashed and limbs were broken. There was fear on both sides, and plenty of it!

It was a lone redcoat sentry who was stationed in front of the Royal Custom House on a cold March eve in 1770 when a group of rowdy Bostonians left the Bunch of Grapes Tavern on King Street (now State Street). Taking advantage of their superior numbers and emboldened by numerous pints of bitter, they began verbally and unmercifully to abuse that British regular. A crowd quickly formed, and the sentry

The Boston Massacre. This famous engraving by Paul Revere depicts British regulars in formation, shooting unarmed Bostonians.
Courtesy of The Bostonian Society.

The Boston Massacre

attempted to retreat, but the Custom House door had been secured for the night. The crowd grew, and so did the ugliness. Soon, the Captain of the Guard, hearing this commotion from a barracks located at the head of King Street, marched a column of redcoats to the perimeter of the mob—now measuring several hundred, many of them armed with clubs—and ordered them to disperse. They refused, and the tension grew, as did the crowd. The news quickly spread, and someone began ringing the bell of the Old Brick Church behind the State House.

We must remember that in the Colonial period, church bells were rung primarily to call the parishioners to services, for special celebrations, or to signal that there was a fire. In the din taking place on State Street, hearing the church bells from afar, many in the mob yelled out, "Fire!"

Well, the redcoats heard what they thought was an order from their captain to fire, and, in absolute fear for their lives, they followed that "order." They fired. They fired into the crowd, killing five Bostonians (including Crispus Attucks, the first black accorded the distinction of "giving his life" in the fight for independence).

It is no wonder, then, that the defending lawyers, John Adams (destined to become the second President of the United States) and Josiah Quincy, were able to get most of these redcoats acquitted by a local jury. Only two of the redcoats did not get off completely: they had their left thumbs branded. They had, in fact, been found guilty of manslaughter, but pleaded benefit of clergy. (Early English and Massachusetts law provided for persons found guilty of manslaughter to read or recite a verse of Scripture and forego prison. To insure that benefit of clergy could only be used once, the guilty party had a thumb branded with the letter M for manslaughter.)

When they left you with the impression that the British, unprovoked, killed unarmed Bostonians, they lied to you—or at least prevaricated.

7

The Boston Tea Party

NOW, ON TO the Boston Tea Party! We are purposely led to think of the Tea Party as a spontaneous result of a public meeting to protest the tax on tea, a meeting where tempers soared due to heated and revolutionary rhetoric. According to this version of history a number of Bostonians, moved by the orators rushed to the waterfront to dump tea into the harbor without any thought of the consequences. This is another lie!

A meeting to protest the tax was, in fact, planned to take place on the evening of December 16, 1773, at Faneuil Hall. But this was not all that had been previously planned. The attack on the three cargo vessels moored at Griffin's Wharf had also been planned and orchestrated in advance. Some of the leaders of the Tea Party met before the planned public meeting, at Benjamin Edes' house, 74 Washington Street. (The punch bowl used for the occasion is today owned by the Massachusetts Historical Society.)

When the crowds trying to get into Faneuil Hall that evening became huge, the decision was made to move the meeting to the larger Old South Meeting House. But, by design, a good number of patriots did not continue directly on to the Old South. Some detoured to the printing offices of Edes and Gill in little Dassett alley off Court Street and there donned their disguises as Mohawk Indians. Others changed their appearances at taverns or private houses throughout the town. At a prearranged signal, which was for Samuel Adams to rise and shout: "This meeting can do nothing more to save the country!" the meeting immediately broke up with cries of "Down to the wharf" by about ninety patriots, mostly in disguise, and they fell in with the mob. At the pier, these "Indians" quietly boarded the three ships and lowered 342 chests of tea in to the harbor.*

It should be noted that not all of the tea made it into the harbor. At least one patriot was discovered trying to smuggle tea, concealed under his shirt and leggings, from the ships for personal consumption; he was tarred and feathered for his misdemeanor. (A bit of this tea taken as evidence is actually on display at the Old State House.)

The disguised participants in this "brave act" remained so secretive as to their identities that historians to this day cannot be certain who the participants were, although you may find a history book or two that claims to identify the participants. One alleged participant supplied a list when he was ninety-three years old. Another recorded his reminiscences seventy-five years after the event, at age 113. John Adams wrote fifty years after the event that he did not know the identity of a single participant.

*These 342 chests contained several tons of tea. But so well orchestrated was this event that the crew on a British frigate anchored not more than five hundred yards away reported neither seeing nor hearing anything unusual that night.

8

The Midnight Ride
of Paul Revere

What's In a Name?

When the lights from the Old North Church flashed out,
Paul Revere was waiting about,
But I was already on my way;
The shadows of night fell cold and gray
As I rode, with never a break or pause.
But what was the use, when my name was Dawes?

History rings with his silvery name;
Closed to me are portals of fame.
Had he been Dawes and I Revere
No one had heard of him, I fear.
No one had heard of me because
He was Revere and I was Dawes.

I am a wandering bitter shade,
Never of me a hero made.
Poets have never sung my praise,
Nobody crowned my head with bays
And if you ask me the fatal cause,
I answer only, "My name is Dawes."

'Tis all very well for the children to hear
Of the midnight ride of Paul Revere;
But why should my name be quite forgot
Who rode as boldly and well, God wot?
Why should I ask? The reason is clear;
My name was Dawes and his Revere.

—Helen F. More

YES, REVERE WAS immortalized by Henry Wadsworth Longfellow with his poem "The Midnight Ride of Paul Revere," and quite properly so, as he was one of the greatest patriots in anybody's history. But in this particular instance, and with due respect, let us set the record straight. In fact, let Paul Revere himself set the record straight.

After the Revolution, the Massachusetts Provincial Congress ordered depositions from all of the eyewitnesses at the battle of Lexington. This was ostensibly to establish that the British had fired first and deliberately. Since Revere's line of vision was blocked when the first shot was fired, his account was not included in the case that the Provincial Congress was preparing. The two depositions that Revere wrote did not come into the hands of the Massachusetts Historical Society until 1920 (donated by the Revere family) and were not published until 1961.

In his own hand Revere states that early in his ride he was almost captured. Later, upon reaching Lexington, he reported to Sam Adams and John Hancock at the Reverend Jonas Clark's house, and was joined by William Dawes. Dawes, you will remember, was the other Son of Liberty who was designated by the patriots to alert the countryside "to arms" once it was determined which route the redcoats were taking. Dawes set off at the same time as Revere, but was assigned a much longer land route from the Boston side of the Charles River through Roxbury. Dawes arrived at the Reverend Clark's house just minutes behind Revere. Revere and Dawes then set off for Concord, where they were joined by Dr. Samuel Prescott. Dr. Prescott was not a part of the original mission. He was returning home from a meeting when Revere and Dawes happened upon him. Knowing Prescott to be another Son of Liberty, they enlisted his aid because he knew the roads and the farms in this area well and was trusted by the residents.

*Part of the first page of Paul Revere's Deposition
regarding his midnight ride, c. 1775.*
Courtesy of the Massachusetts Historical Society.

All three men were then captured by another redcoat patrol. Dawes and Prescott managed to escape, but this time Revere did not escape and was detained for an unspecified length of time. He was finally released without his horse, and he returned on foot to the Reverend Clark's house where he rejoined Adams and Hancock. In the

The Midnight Ride of Paul Revere

meantime, Dawes and Prescott continued to "alert the countryside," insuring that the minutemen would make it to Concord in time to confront the British there.

The history books never even mentioned the name of Revere until after his death, which was fifty years after the event. The Longfellow poem, in 1863, changed history, and in more ways than one. For example, the poem says, "one if by land, and two if by sea. . . ." Everyone remembers from Longfellow's poem that two lanterns (made, in fact, by Revere himself) were hung from the steeple of the Old North Church, so many assume that the British set out for Lexington by sea. Actually, they had been camped on Boston Common, and they embarked in boats with muffled oars from what is now the corner of Boylston and Charles streets to cross over to Cambridge; this area had yet to be filled in and then was part of the Charles River estuary. The British started by water, yes. But certainly not by sea! Perhaps no one ever told you as well that Longfellow's poem was written in a propaganda effort to inspire northerners to enlist in the War Between the States.

The two lanterns, not so incidentally, are the reason that the Old West Church on Cambridge Street does not have a proper steeple. The British commanding general, Thomas Gage, to insure that the rebels could never use *this* church steeple to send lantern signals, ordered his troops to chop it off. After the Revolution was won, Bostonians never rebuilt the steeple. They simply topped the church with a cupola as a reminder that the wicked British even desecrated the Colonists' churches.

As a final footnote to this chapter of our history, one other detail should also be mentioned. Historians agree that after outrunning the first British patrol that tried to capture him, Revere hastened first to Medford. There he met with Isaac Hull. Hull was renowned as a distiller of "Medford Rum." But why historians always seem to report that Revere stopped at Hull's Tavern and then describe Hull as the famous distiller of Medford Rum, rather than as Captain Hull, the commanding officer of the local minutemen, we leave to the imagination of the reader.

9

The Battle of
Bunker Hill

ONLY IN BOSTON would one find a 221-foot Egyptian obelisk built to commemorate a battle that the patriots *lost*. And, if that weren't enough, the Bostonians went and got the name of the hill wrong.

In the first place, the hill now known around the world is actually *Bunker's Hill*, not Bunker Hill. It was named for its owner George Bunker. When patriot spies learned that the British were planning to fortify Bunker's Hill, they hurried under cover of darkness to get there first, and in fact, they did fortify a hill on June 16, 1775. However, the hill they actually fortified was *Breed's Hill*, not Bunker's Hill.

No one knows for certain why the patriots fortified the wrong hill. The error may have been a result of using stolen British maps that referred to all three of Charlestown's hills as Bunker Hill. Or it simply could have been the result of most of the patriots being from out of town and not knowing one hill from another, especially at night. (Military historians argue that Breed's Hill was simply the best of the three hills to defend.)

The true Bunker's Hill is actually a half mile to the northwest of Breed's Hill, and is the present site of Saint Francis de Sales Church. The "Battle of Bunker Hill" took place, and the monument stands, on Breed's Hill.

Although the colonists repulsed the first two British charges, on the third attempt the redcoats won the hill. The victory was pyrrhic, though, as British losses totaled 1,054, versus 441 patriots killed. As soon as the king was informed, he immediately fired his Commanding General Thomas Gage. (Thereafter, Gage was derided in England as "Lord Lexington, the Baron of Bunker Hill.")

The cornerstone of the Bunker Hill Monument was set by General Marquis de Lafayette on July 17, 1825. Lafayette took with him several steamer trunks of earth from Breed's hill, soil which now surrounds his grave in Paris. Due to lack of funds, the monument was not completed until 1843. Remarkably, even with an eighteen-year delay, it was dedicated on both occasions by Daniel Webster.

Once considered "America's Monument," the Bunker Hill Monument was superseded after the Civil War by the completion of the Washington Monument, which is today the preeminent American monument in the minds of all but Bostonians. No matter how high the monument ranks in your own mind, remember that it doesn't stand on Bunker Hill!

10

Trimountaine

WE LEARNED earlier that John Winthrop discovered William Blaxton living at the base of one of the peninsula's three original hills, now called Beacon Hill. What no one probably told you, though, is that the streets on this section of the hill were named as a historical reflection of this Anglican minister's early plantings (estimated at three to six acres). Consider:

Garden Street

Grove Street

West Cedar Street

Acorn Street

Branch Street

Chestnut Street

Willow Street

Walnut Street

Myrtle Street

Cedar Lane Way

Fruit Street

Blossom Street

The Hancock House, on Beacon Street at the top of Beacon Hill.
Courtesy of the Boston Public Library Print Department.

These original three hills had extremely steep peaks. So steep, in fact, that to build on the Beacon Street side was all but impossible. To reach the peaks of all three hills from their north slopes, rope walks were necessary. Contrary to popular misconception, wealthy Bostonians did not inhabit the tops of these hills until the nineteenth century. The notable exception was the Hancock family, whose mansion was next to the present State House on Beacon Hill. The lower north slope (on the Cambridge Street side) was a Negro section, and the area near what is now Charles Circle was a notorious red-light district.

The westernmost hill was eventually named Mount Vernon, but for almost half a century, because of this longstanding red-light district, Bostonians called it Mount Whoredom. The easternmost hill was originally named Cotton Hill after the family who first settled the base (approximately at Tremont and Beacon streets); later it was changed to Pemberton Hill and is today the site of the Pemberton Square Court House. The middle, tallest, hill was first called Sentry Hill. It was Sentry because, until it was flattened to make way for the

Bulfinch State House, Bostonians posted at this peak a twenty-four-hour sentry with a long bamboo pole and a bucket of pitch. His responsibility, if the town should come under attack, was to light the tar and hoist the bucket to signal the militia and citizens to defend the city.

As Boston began to grow and prosper and lack of land was proving to be a serious constraint, the hills were ultimately leveled (Sentry Hill in 1795, Mount Vernon in 1803, Pemberton in 1835) to provide earth for new landfill and to provide flatter, buildable land. Sentry Hill was then renamed Beacon Hill.

If they told you that the earth from these hills was used to create the Back Bay, once again they lied to you. Most of the earth from Mount Vernon was used to create Charles Street. The earth from Pemberton Hill was used to create what is today Leverett Circle and part of the West End. The fill from the top of Sentry Hill created most of the North Station area.

II

More on Streets

IN 1789 George Washington paid his last visit to Boston. He was here for nearly a week, and citizens came from all over New England and as far away as New York to pay homage to the great general who had just become our first president. There were parades daily in his honor, stately dinners each evening, and fireworks every night on Boston Common. After he departed, residents throughout the town petitioned the City Council to have the name of *their* street changed to Washington Street. There were so many requests, in fact, that Boston officials met with state officials, and together they decided to solve the dilemma by creating a Washington Street starting in Boston and making it the longest street in the commonwealth. Over the years, they did just that. Although they never told you, Washington Street begins at the Charlestown Bridge and does not end until it actually reaches Rhode Island!

But the Boston officials, suspecting that over time literally every city and town in the United States would name a major thoroughfare after the first president, decided to ensure that Boston would be forever unique. By decree, within the City of Boston, every street (with a handful of exceptions), as it crosses over Washington Street must (in honor of George Washington) change its name! For example:

Court Street becomes *State* Street

Winter Street becomes *Summer* Street

Boylston Street becomes *Essex* Street

Stuart Street becomes *Kneeland* Street

Berkeley Street becomes *East Berkeley* Street

West Newton Street becomes *East Newton* Street, etc.

Initially, two important exceptions were made (for obvious reasons): Massachusetts Avenue and Columbus Avenue. Neither has to change its name as it crosses over Washington Street. More recently, and after considerable reflection by the city council, when Melnea Cass Boulevard was built, it too was exempted from changing its name as it crosses over Washington Street. This great and unprecedented honor paid by Boston to a great lady from Roxbury who did so much for her community for so many years* has gone unnoticed even by black historians. In fact, even Melnea Cass's grandchildren were unaware of this exemption and its historical significance until this writer made it known to WBZ-TV news reporter Sarah-Ann Shaw, who in turn informed the grandchildren.

---

* Melnea Cass began her lifelong civil rights activities in 1919 with the Women's Suffrage Movement. She founded Roxbury's Freedom House in 1974. Mayor Kevin H. White included her on his 1976 list of seven distinguished "grand Bostonians." The First Lady of Roxbury was among the local dignitaries introduced to Queen Elizabeth II when the English monarch visited Boston during the Bicentennial celebration in 1976.

More on Streets

12

Even More On Streets That They didn't Tell You

STATE STREET originally was *King* Street, as you've already read, and *Court* Street was *Queen* Street; *Court* Square was *Prisoner* Lane, since it was the location of the first jailhouse. It was there that Bostonians held the infamous Captain Kidd, in 1699, before he was sent to London to be tried, found guilty of piracy, and hanged.

The portion of *Boylston* Street along Boston Common was originally *Frogg* Lane. (The frogs in the Common and along the Charles River estuary were reportedly over a foot long.) The name was changed to honor Zabdiel Boylston for inoculating Bostonians against smallpox.

Many of the street names originally acknowledged then obvious features which have since disappeared. For example: *Spring* Lane, *Water* Street, *High* Street, *Beach* Street, *Batterymarch* Street, *Causeway* Street, and *Temple* Place. The great spring that provided fresh water for over two centuries is covered over. Water Street no longer ends at the water since the original shoreline was filled in. (Long Wharf, in fact, was originally two thousand feet long and ended at the base of the Custom House. Basically, everything east of the Custom House was originally the ocean.) There is no longer any hill at High Street. No beach remains (nor ocean) at the end of Beach Street. The causeway has been filled in, and the battery (fortification) has been long since torn down. Boston's first Masonic Temple, at the corner of Temple Place and Tremont Street, has been torn down also.

Many other street names refer to early property owners or local notables such as *Hancock, Winthrop, Revere,* and Governor John *Endicott.* Others so honored include *Louis Prang,* who printed the first Christmas cards in the United States; John *Hull,* who minted the first coins in the Colonies, and Jacob *Sleeper,* a founder of Boston University.

Purchase Street was named in spite of the original property owner. Boston, being a leader in shipbuilding for a time, was also the rope-making capital of the country. One local maker of rope, John Harrison, owned property along what was then the waterfront (by Pearl and Oliver streets) in a location that was convenient for people traveling from Church Green (now Summer and Bedford streets) to the ocean-front. They used his property as a shortcut, much to his anger, and he dearly enjoyed stringing his ropes to dry in such a way as to block carts

The corner of Congress and Purchase streets, 1860.
Courtesy of the Boston Public Library Print Department.

Even More On Streets That They Didn't Tell You

and pedestrians. The locals complained so often to town officials that the city finally purchased the property to make it a public way. And eschewing a common custom of naming a street after an owner deprived of property through eminent domain, they simply named it Purchase Street!

Of course, many streets were simply named out of nostalgia for the settlers' original homeland or to honor famous personages in England. For example, all of the alphabetical cross streets in the Back Bay were named in honor of British lords, dukes, and earls:

Arlington

Berkeley

Clarendon

Dartmouth

Exeter

Fairfield

Gloucester

Hereford

Likewise, the two east-west streets: Marlborough and Newbury.

Although most persons know that these streets run alphabetically, you may not know that the alphabetical scheme continues well into the Fenway district! In the Fenway, although not quite in the organized pattern of the Back Bay, we find:

Ipswich

Jersey

Kilmarnock

Landsdowne

Museum Road

Newbury Street Extension

Overland

Peterboro

Queensbury

In Boston's South End, the reasoning behind street names was also logical, but different. When the South Station Railway Terminal was completed in 1899, it was the largest station in the world. It then rapidly became one of the busiest in the world! Trains arrived and departed around the clock, 365 days a year, to and from distant points in the West and the South. In 1915, over 34 million passengers used the South Station, making this terminal the busiest in the world at that time. (Boston's North Station was the second busiest, with twenty-nine million, and Grand Central in New York City was third, with twenty-five million.)

The closest major street to South Station, which runs parallel to the railroad tracks, is *Albany*, named for a destination reached from that station. But they never told you that over sixty percent of the original streets in the South End also were named for train destinations. Consider the following streets:

Dover (now East Berkeley)

Stoughton

Canton

Sharon (now the driveway to the Boston University Medical Center's Doctor's Office Building at 720 Harrison Avenue)

Newton

Concord

Worcester

Springfield

Wareham

Holyoke

Dedham

Brookline

Randolph

Plympton

Northampton

Lenox

Even More On Streets That They Didn't Tell You

Groton

Milford

Hanson

Upton

Pelham

Southhampton

Waltham

Bristol

Hampden

Yarmouth

Rutland

Greenwich

Pembroke

(New) Haven

Camden

Savoy

Finally, regarding presidents and streets of Boston, Boston has a street named for every president up to and including President Harry S Truman, with the following five exceptions:

James Monroe

Millard Fillmore

Herbert Hoover

Theodore Roosevelt

Franklin Roosevelt

13

Jaywalking on the Streets of Boston

THEY MAY HAVE told you that Boston is the Jaywalking Capital of the United States, but they never told you why. Again, let's start with some background.

Remember that in the Colonial era, Boston was a tiny peninsula, somewhat pear-shaped (with two bites taken out of it) with very little land to it (see the Bonner map on page 8). In fact, Boston (at high tide) consisted of two islands. The North End was actually separated from the peninsula by a break along what is now approximately Blackstone Street, making it a tiny isle. To reach the North End, one had to cross a footbridge. The peninsula itself was connected to Roxbury by a narrow causeway called Boston Neck. At high tides the water would frequently spill over the neck and also turn Boston into an island unto itself!

Boston, then, was so small that its residents had little need for horses, wagons, and carriages. Distances were so short that people usually walked wherever they were going. As a result, there were footpaths everywhere—from house to house, to the churches, taverns, and markets, to the waterfront and the wharves. And these footpaths meandered around and over brooks, streams, boulders, trees, and other natural obstacles that today no longer exist, creating the unplanned pattern reminiscent of old cities in Europe.

As mentioned earlier, when Boston began to really grow and prosper, lack of land proved to be a major handicap. The hills were leveled to provide flatter areas to build on and to generate new landfill. The waterfront area was filled in, as was part of the West End and so was the Charles Street area.

Then, with financial incentives from the government, two major private landfill projects were accomplished. The first was the filling in of South Cove, begun in 1833, to create the present-day South End district. The second, the largest single landfill project in history of the United States, was the Back Bay Landfill Project. Begun in 1857, this project required the building of a railroad line approximately from today's Back Bay Station ten miles west to Needham Heights. It was the hills of Needham that provided the landfill for the Back Bay. With the tremendous influx of cheap labor to Boston (especially the Irish escaping the potato famine), this reclamation project went on, twenty-four hours a day, seven days a week, for forty years. The Back Bay was not completed, in terms of buildings, until 1910—overall, a sixty-year effort of filling and building!

During this period, Boston also went on an acquisition binge, annexing virtually all of the surrounding contiguous towns, making them districts of the city—South Boston in 1804; Roxbury in 1868; Dorchester in 1870; West Roxbury in 1872; Charlestown in 1873; Brighton in 1874; and Hyde Park in 1912. Commonwealth Avenue from the Cottage Farm Bridge (now the Boston University Bridge), was acquired from Brookline in 1874. Most of what is today the Allston district was part of Cambridge, and this was also purchased by Boston. The only contiguous town which would not agree to annexation was Brookline; the Brookline newspaper headlines of the day screamed, "We will not be *Suffolk-kated*." (Boston, of course, is in Suffolk County, and Brookline in Norfolk.) As a consequence, Brookline today may not be "suffolkated," but it is certainly surrounded on three sides by Boston.

As soon as there were substantial distances to travel within the city (it changed from a town to a city in 1822), horses, wagons, carts, and carriages became necessities. So the old, narrow, crooked, winding footpaths were cobblestoned for the better purchase of the horses' hooves. Then, when the automobile came along, they paved over the cobblestones. Hence, in all of the original sections of the city and the original sections of annexed districts as well, drivers are negotiating paved-over footpaths.

In the Bostonian collective unconscious, they are *still* footpaths and are primarily for the use of pedestrians. Motorized vehicles be damned! This is part of every Bostonian's gene pool, *and will always be*. This is not uncommon in our older eastern cities. Many cities acquired character traits very early on which remain true to this day. Consider, for example, the entry in Samuel Adams' journal regarding his first—and last—visit to New York City in 1774. Only two succinct sentences! "I have never been in such a busy and bustling city. I have never met such rude people!" On the other hand, however boorish one may be to a resident of Atlanta, the Atlantean will always be most polite and gracious in return—although later he may go home and kick the cat! (Mysteriously, newcomers to such cities always seem to acquire those character defining genes almost immediately.)

So, if they told you that the streets of Boston were a result of cowpaths, they told you another lie. There was, in fact, a major cowpath leading from the Common (West Street) to Pond Street (now Bedford Street), where the cattle were watered. There was also a short cowpath from Spruce Street to the Common. But livestock generally grazed on Boston Common, on the Neck, or in pastures owned by the wealthy. Cows typically were just not allowed to wander about.

Since we happened to mention islands in this section, it may be appropriate here to point out another fact they likely never told you: Logan International Airport was originally Boston Airport on an island in Boston Harbor. It used to be Bird's Island, from which one had to take a ferry to Boston upon landing. Through more landfill expansion, the airport ultimately swallowed up Apple Island and Governor's Island. And, of course, they never told you that East Boston was Noddle's Island (originally home to one family, the Noddles, who raised cows; Mr. Noddle would row across the harbor daily to sell his milk in the North End). Eventually, both the airport islands and Noddle's Island were linked together, finally joining up with the mainland. (See the map on page 10).

14

Liberty Square

ON JANUARY 24, 1793, one of the biggest, longest, and rowdiest parties in the history of Boston took place. It began in what was then a residential (now commercial) area of the city, at the intersection of Kilby, Water, and Batterymarch streets. The celebration was in honor of the French Revolution.

Bostonians recognize and will be ever grateful for the fact that without the assistance of the French, American Independence might never have been achieved. Most fondly remembered and revered is the Marquis de Lafayette. He withdrew his commission from the military service of his own country in 1777 and came to the Colonies in his own ship to volunteer his services to General George Washington in any capacity and without pay. Most Bostonians know that the city has named Avenue de Lafayette and Lafayette Place in his honor, as well as Fayette Court and Fayette Street. But even Bostonians have never been told that LaGrange Street, between Boylston and Stuart streets in the downtown theater district, LaGrange Place in Roxbury, and LaGrange Street in West Roxbury also honor General Lafayette. LaGrange, you see, was the marquis' summer estate in the south of France.

When Lafayette toured what were the original thirteen states in his final visit to America (after laying the cornerstone of the Bunker Hill Monument in 1824), the crowds were, in many instances, larger than when President George Washington made his final tour in 1789. Even now, every year on July 14, Boston closes down a section of Marlboro Street near the French Library and celebrates Bastille Day. A stately dinner of *haute cuisine* is followed by dancing until the wee hours, both indoors and out.

Back in 1793, these feelings were even more pronounced than they are today, and they were universally shared. So when the news arrived that the French were close to winning their own liberty, equality, and fraternity, a spontaneous emotion of kindred spirit exploded in Boston.

An ox weighing over one thousand pounds was barbecued somewhere nearby, hoisted onto a wagon, and brought to the open area where Kilby, Water, and Batterymarch streets intersected. Someone mounted the ox horns on a sixty-foot rod and raised a "liberty pole" to the French. Another cart appeared carrying eight hundred loaves of bread, then still another loaded with hogsheads of very potent punch. The revelers then decided to parade through the entire city and stop at the homes of Governor John Hancock, Lieutenant Governor Samuel Adams, and anyone else they could think of with whom to raise a toast of good cheer. The parade lasted all day and well into the next morning. It was estimated that fully one half of the population got drunk also.

When the French Revolution ended, Bostonians in their euphoria declared the confluence of the three streets to be Liberty Square. Unfortunately, over the years, later generations have forgotten this unprecedented event in their history and in ignorance have associated Liberty Square with American independence, not with the French Revolution.

And in 1992 the city decided to honor (and rightly so) the freedom fighters in Hungary. By this time, even the Boston officials might not have known that Liberty Square was designated specifically in honor of the French, for instead of choosing some previously unspoken-for location, they placed a statue dedicated to "Those who never surrendered, October 1956, Hungary" in the middle of (French) Liberty Square. This decision might have, in the normal course of events, erased forever the square's connection with the French Revolution. However, now that *you* have been told, perhaps this wonderful episode in Boston's rich history will not be irrevocably lost.

Liberty Square

15

The Society of Friends: The Quakers

CONSULT ANY ENCYCLOPEDIA and you will discover that the Society of Friends was begun in England by George Fox in 1648. Fox rejected formality in religion, believing that every person could find truth by recognizing for himself the divine spirit in his own being—"the Light within." Fox founded groups in England, on the continent of Europe, and even found followers in Jamaica and the Barbados. The name Quakers was given to the group in derision by Gervase Bennett, a magistrate at Derby, England, when Fox called on the official to "tremble in the name of the Lord."

Adherents of this sect were first noticed in Boston in 1656, "quaking and trembling at the word of God." They set up a modest meeting house on the corner of Salter's Court in Congress Square. Their mission was to save the superstitious colony of Massachusetts with a message from the Lord, i.e., to fight against superstition and priestology. Actually, their mere presence would have been cause for the intolerant Puritans to persecute the Quakers. But the Society of Friends' call for the disuse of any outward ordinances of baptism and the Lord's Supper, and for the discontinuance of a salaried ministry and of tithes, enraged the locals. Furthermore, the Quakers would not remove their hats in the presence of superiors, would always use the familiar form of address (*thee* and *thou*), would never take an oath even if required in court, and would not bend knee even to the king himself. Needless to say, this caused tremendous difficulties for the sect.

As a result, these first Quakers were jailed, had their books burned, and were finally sent to Barbados. As more arrived to replace those banished, they were accorded the same treatment, now to include fines and whipping. Undaunted, Quakers continued to stream into Boston.

In 1657, The General Court passed new, harsher laws specifically to deal with these heretics. Any man convicted of being a Quaker was to have an ear cut off. A woman was stripped and publicly whipped for her first conviction. For a second conviction, she, too, was to lose an ear. The second conviction for a man meant the loss of his other ear. Whether male or female, the third conviction carried the penalty of having one's tongue pierced with a red-hot iron! If, after all this, a Quaker still would not leave, or returned from Barbados, he or she would be sold into slavery.

But, incredibly, return they did! So in 1658, the Puritans legislated the ultimate penalty. Any banished Quaker who returned to Boston would be put to death. By 1660, four Quakers were hanged for returning, the last being Mary Dyer. She was executed on Boston Neck, four hundred feet south of Dover Street on the east side of what is today Washington Street.

Nevertheless, more Quakers kept arriving, and they continued to be persecuted. By now, however, word of the atrocities had spread back to England and eventually reached the ear of King Charles II. Charles II was not a particularly tolerant monarch, but he sent a mandate to the Puritan leaders in Boston that they immediately cease and desist. You will, of course, remember that Charles II's father, Charles I, was brought to trial and had his death warrant signed by Oliver Cromwell. What you may not remember is that Cromwell was a Puritan!

In 1689, the Toleration Act was passed in England by the Parliament, and this edict took all of the pressure off the Quakers in Boston. In 1694, they were actually able to purchase land on Brattle Street (in what is today's Government Center) and build their first church. This church, in fact, was the first church in Boston ever made of brick. As fantastic as it sounds, once the Quakers were finally being tolerated in Boston—able to acquire property, to build churches and to worship in peace—their numbers immediately began to dwindle. Their congregation had grown in Boston, ironically, only under persecution!

In 1710 they moved to Congress Street, to a much smaller church, where they established a cemetery. In 1744, there were only eleven Quakers left in all of Boston. By 1808, the society became extinct and Boston was Quakerless. Finally, in 1827, the church site and cemetery were sold and the bodies disinterred and removed to Lynn, Massachusetts.

All of this has been well documented over the years as an ignominious part of Boston's history. And even though we will now underline the fact that the Puritans always offered the Quakers total immunity if they would only go, it in no way lessens the horror of their deeds. But what is also interesting is what they never told you about the early Quakers.

Today, many have a great admiration for this religious body distinguished by mystical devotion, silent worship, rejection of ritual and formulas. They are respected for their refusal to sanction violence and war as well as their well-known humanitarianism. But in what was the first stage of an evolution culminating in their present respected status, "some of their eccentricities (according to noted historian George Weston) today would not be tolerated even by barbarians!"

In early Colonial Boston it seems that Quakers would never cut their hair. They would frequently blacken their faces with charcoal and prance naked in the streets. This was during the day! At night they would run through the town smashing bottles, urinating in public, and shrieking in high-pitched voices. (One has to wonder if their even more barbaric treatment by the Puritans drove the Quakers to some of these acts.)

Today, Boston has only two tangible reminders of these early Quakers. The first is a statue of Mary Dyer on Beacon Hill by the State House, seen by hundreds of thousands annually. The second, however, is almost always overlooked by visitors and usually unrecognized by residents. It is Quaker Lane, which is totally unique in a town otherwise famous for its myriad of crooked, narrow streets. Directly south, opposite the Old State House, Quaker Lane is not three hundred yards long. Its uniqueness lies in the fact that it crosses itself at approximately right angles: from 29 State Street and 46 Devonshire Street, to 15 and 25 Congress Street. This lane has then, in fact, four entrances!

This configuration represents the remains of the original paths of the old Quaker Cemetery, whose occupants were long ago disinterred and removed to Lynn.

16

The Castle

MAYBE THEY DID tell you that the Park Plaza Castle at the corner of Columbus Avenue and Arlington Street was originally the First Corps of Cadets Armory. They may even have mentioned that prior to its acquisition by the Park Plaza Hotel, the castle was used by the Boston school system for junior high school basketball games. But the truth as to who built this castle and why it was built is yet another skeleton in Boston's closet. Again, some historical background is needed.

Originally, being so small—approximately three miles long and no more than one mile at its widest — Boston had only one real residential area. Regardless of class, just about everybody in the town lived in or about the North End, due primarily to the freshwater spring located nearby. By the end of the eighteenth century, however, well-born Bostonians and those successful in business were anxious to leave the rough, teeming North End for better housing (which would also better reflect their social station). So, in 1795, America's first professional architect, Charles Bulfinch, designed and built the first block of connected residences, or townhouses, in Boston. Called the Tontine Crescent, it was on Franklin Street (which Bulfinch was given the privilege of naming and did so in honor of his greatest hero, Benjamin Franklin) between Hawley and Devonshire streets. In the center of the crescent was an arch over a way that led to Summer Street. (Although

Charles Bullfinch's Tontine Crescent, on Franklin Street, 1855.
The archway is visible on the right of the picture.
Courtesy of the Boston Public Library Print Department.

the Tontine was torn down in 1858, today's Arch Street marks the location of the original archway that can be seen in the photo.)

By the beginning of the nineteenth century, more and more arrivals from Europe put even more pressure on the already-crowded North End. So, in 1814, Bulfinch designed the New South Church at the junction of Summer and Bedford streets. Around it, he designed and built another residential area called Church Green. (The street sign here still says Church Green!) It became the most beautiful residential area in Boston, and perhaps in the entire country. The homes (some were magnificent mansions), in a relatively pastoral setting within sight of the ocean, were complemented by some of the most beautiful gardens in the land. (America's first horticultural society had its origin right in Church Green.) So it was here that the wealthiest would graciously live, a safer distance from the overpopulated North End. Meanwhile, the North End grew even more over-

The Castle

Aftermath of the Fire of 1872—Pearl Street.
Courtesy of the Boston Public Library Print Department.

crowded by the middle of the nineteenth century, when the Irish began arriving in ever increasing numbers to escape starvation.

Still later in the century, The Fire—another thing they probably never told you about—again redistributed Boston's wealthy. In 1872, one year after the Great Chicago Fire, Boston experienced an even greater fire. (This has been long since forgotten because it didn't start with a story about Mrs. O'Leary's cow kicking over a lantern.) The Great Boston Fire began in a warehouse on Lincoln Street and raged uncontrolled for over twenty hours. Every fire company in Massachusetts responded, and were it not for a pressurized fire engine sent by rail from Portsmouth, New Hampshire, the entire city probably would have been lost. As it was, the fire was finally contained at the foot of School Street at Washington Street. (Miraculously, the North End was not affected.) The Old South Meeting House, which had started to burn, was saved. But over one quarter of the original downtown area, including Church Green, was totally destroyed. Now, with the Back Bay reclamation project in full gear, the Boston Brahmins had three choices: they could rebuild their homes at Church Green, they

The Park Plaza Castle, formerly the First
Corps of Cadets Armory.
From the author's collection.

The Castle

could relocate to this new Back Bay district, or they could move to the now buildable Beacon Hill area. (Although the South Cove landfill project, which created the South End was completed at this time, it never attracted the "well-born" Bostonians.) Since (according to Boston's Yankees) even more of these "uncultivated, unskilled, poor Irish Catholic 'vermin' were infesting the North End" than ever before, the Brahmins opted to relocate even further away and went to Beacon Hill and the Back Bay.

However, these upper-class Bostonians were not totally comforted by just putting more distance between themselves and the Irish. They were convinced that it was just a matter of time before this "rabble" would start an uprising against them and confiscate their wealth. To protect themselves against this "inevitable" uprising, in 1891 the Yankees built a fortress. They built a drymoat around it, with a drawbridge to get in and out, and they stocked it with arms and ammunition. The feared uprising, of course, never occurred. Today the moat is gone, but the drawbridge is still there. The fort, originally named the First Corps of Cadets Armory, is now called the Park Plaza Castle.

A final note regarding Charles Bulfinch, one that they never told you: Although Benjamin H. Latrobe had been responsible for designing the Capitol in Washington, D.C., he was having great difficulty with the Washington Commissioner of Buildings while trying to rebuild what the British had burned in 1814. He finally resigned in 1817. Latrobe was replaced by Bulfinch, who redesigned and completed our magnificent Capitol building.

17

Henry Hobson Richardson, Fredric Auguste Bartholdi, and the Statue of Liberty

AFTER GRADUATING from Harvard, H.H. Richardson went to Paris, and passed the entrance examinations to L'Ecole des Beaux Arts on his second attempt. For the next five years, 1860–65, he studied architecture under the famous Henri Labrouste. It was here that he first crossed paths with Frederic Auguste Bartholdi, another student.

The next time they were to meet would be 1871 in New York. Bartholdi looked up his old school acquaintance on this, his first visit to America. He had already conceived his statue of Liberty and had come to the United States to learn more about us and, in particular, the political climate regarding acceptance of such a bold gift. In "talking shop," Richardson heard about Bartholdi's statue idea, and Bartholdi in turn learned of Richardson's current project, the Brattle Square Church of Boston.

The church, located at the corner of Commonwealth Avenue and Clarendon Street, was to be purchased later and renamed by the First Baptist Church upon its relocation from the South End. Richardson, perhaps the best United States architect to build with massive granite blocks, was not particularly accomplished in fine detail work. From the base of this Romanesque church, however, he envisioned a tall Florentine tower with bas-relief carvings depicting baptism, Communion, marriage, and death. He knew that he needed help for that kind of intricate detail at the top of the tower, and that this was Bartholdi's forte. So he commissioned Bartholdi to do the relief statues representing the Angels of Judgment blowing golden trumpets. (Bostonians today refer to these angels as the beanblowers!)

Bartholdi went back to Paris and spent more time on the Statue of Liberty project than on the work commissioned by his friend Richardson. In fact, the frieze was not delivered to Boston until 1877, five years after it had been commissioned! This caused a strain between the two architects that may have proved very costly to Boston, as we shall soon see.

On his first United States visit Bartholdi, immediately upon

*The First Baptist Church, at the corner of
Commonwealth Avenue and Clarendon Street.*
From the author's collection.

entering the port of New York, had recognized Bedloe's Island as the perfect place for his Liberty statue. For several years, formalities were negotiated among France, the City of New York, and the Federal government, which owned the island. A great deal of public relations work was attempted over ten years to keep the United States interest alive. After the Americans' initial curiosity over the idea here, interest slowly waned over the years to the point of skepticism and finally scant notice. When the statue was finally completed in 1883 and presented to United States officials in Paris in 1884, New Yorkers realized for the first time that, although they were getting the statue for free, they were expected to pay for building a base and for erecting the statue! New Yorkers considered this to be a terrible affront and would not (or could not) raise the necessary funds.

So, even though their relationship was still strained over the several-year delay in completing the First Baptist Church bas-relief, Bartholdi made it known to Richardson that Boston Harbor could have the statue if Bostonians could quickly raise the funds for construction of the base and erection of the statue. It turns out, however, that Bartholdi was using this old (and shaky) friendship as an elaborate ploy. He desperately wanted the Statue on Bedloe Island and gambled that when New Yorkers discovered the "offer" to Boston, they would quickly respond by raising the necessary monies. In fact, the same overture was made to Philadelphia! The gambit worked magnificently; within days the funds were raised in New York.

Had their friendship and trust been as strong as it was back in 1871, it is very possible that Bartholdi would have simply said, "To hell with those New Yorkers," and the Statue of Liberty would have been in Boston Harbor. Significantly, even though Richardson bid on the base for the statue, he did not receive the commission. (Architectural historians almost unanimously agree that Richardson was the man for the job and would have created a base fittingly complementary for this magnificent work of art.)

But, although they never told you, Boston does have one of the few works on mainland America done by Bartholdi—the frieze at the top of the First Baptist Church.

Richardson, of course, went on to build Trinity Church in Copley Square, which has been recognized by architects, past and present, to be the best church ever built in America from an architectural

---

*A close-up of the First Baptist Church north side bas-relief:
Communion. The central figure is a likeness of Henry
Wadsworth Longfellow. The two male figures at the left are
Ralph Waldo Emerson and Nathaniel Hawthorne.*
Courtesy of The Bostonian Society.

standpoint, and one of the seven best buildings in any category ever
built in the United States.

(While we are focused on Trinity Church, we bet that they never
told you that the Reverend Phillips Brooks, its first pastor and a close
friend of Richardson's, wrote for his catechism class the Christmas
hymn "O Little Town of Bethlehem.")

As it turned out there was somewhat of a quid pro quo: It was
Richardson and Brooks who invited a New Yorker to bid on develop-
ing a new park system for Boston. Frederick Law Olmsted, who had
just finished his first commission, New York's Central Park, came to
Boston in 1898 and ended up designing the famous Emerald Necklace
that runs from the Public Garden to Franklin Park. He stayed here for
the rest of his life, designing public and private parks as well as estates
all over North America. He became recognized as the "father of
landscape architecture." (Boston loses some, and it wins some!)

There is one more little-known footnote to this chapter of our
history: Bartholdi later confided to a friend, historian Edward Everett
Hale, that the figures on the tower of the First Baptist Church are,
in fact, likenesses of distinguished men. Some of those depicted include William Lloyd Garrison, Charles Sumner, Edward Everett,
Wendell Phillips, Henry Wadsworth Longfellow, Ralph Waldo
Emerson, and Nathaniel Hawthorne.

18

Words and Phrases Coined in Boston

EVER SINCE JOHN HULL, America's first mintmaster, coined the Pine Tree Shilling in Boston in 1652, Bostonians have played a significant role in the coining process. At least, that is, in the coining of words and phrases that have become a part of the English language.

Blue Laws. As we have already learned, a large number of the laws enacted in early Boston were, to say the least, restrictive. The town officials, following the tradition of the English Parliament, ordered these official acts to be printed on blue paper. Hence the term Blue Laws, which was first used derogatorily in 1781 and has kept that connotation ever since.

Uncle Tom. Harriet Beecher Stowe, daughter of Lyman Beecher (pastor of the Bowdoin Street Congregational Church—now the Mission Church of St. John the Evangelist), lived at 42 Green Street from 1826 to 1832. This was when she ex-perienced her religious conversion and where the seeds of her famous book, *Uncle Tom's Cabin,* began to grow.

Columbia River. In 1787, Bostonian Joseph Barrell organized the first expedition to the Northwest Territory (then continuing around the world!). This voyage established American claims to the Oregon Territory. There, under the command of Captain Robert Gray, the explorers sailed into a great river, which they named the Columbia after their ship.

Black Maria. Maria Lee was a black woman who operated a run-down transient hotel in Boston. Frequently, she would turn in drunken and criminal customers, often physically helping the police with their arrests. In the early part of the twentieth century, making fun of the Irish was becoming "politically incorrect," and the so-called paddy wagon, which was used to haul offenders to jail, was renamed the Black Maria.

Gerrymander. In 1812, Governor Elbridge Gerry (who was later vice president under James Madison) exhibited a map on which he shrewdly indicated how certain districts could be reapportioned in a way greatly to his own political advantage. When the great Boston painter Gilbert Stuart saw the map, he noticed a resemblance to the body of an elongated animal. He added a head, claws, and wings, remarking, "That will do for a salamander." When he hung it in his editor's office, the editor growled, "Salamander, hell! Better to call it a Gerrymander."

Hooker. Major General "Fighting Joe" Hooker's statue next to the state house on Beacon Hill is passed by hundreds of thousands annually. Historians remember his defeat at the hands of General Robert E. Lee at Chancellorsville in 1863, though Hooker had two-to-one superiority in numbers. (Again, Bostonians honored defeat

Charles Street Jail horse-drawn van, c. 1920. Once called "paddy wagons," these conveyances were later known as Black Marias.
Courtesy of the Boston Public Library Print Department.

What They Never Told You About Boston

with a monument.) During the Civil War, "Fighting Joe" allowed women to follow his troops in their own tent encampments, and they eventually got the name, Hooker's Ladies.

Nigger heaven. In Christ Church, now known as the famous "Old North Church," the balcony above the church organ was built for occupancy by slaves. From this yet another racial epithet was born.

Boston Brahmin. Dr. Oliver Wendell Holmes published a series of articles in the *Atlantic Monthly* called "Autocrat of the Breakfast Table." Here, he coined the term Boston Brahmin.

Muckrakers. As a student at Harvard, Theodore Roosevelt read Bunyan's *Pilgrim's Progress*. From the character who was so intent on raking up muck that he didn't observe that a heavenly halo was being held over his head, President Roosevelt years later coined the term *muckrakers*.

John. The first reference to calling a bathroom a "john" appeared in print in 1753. The official regulations of Harvard College that year read, "No freshman shall go to the Fellow's Cousin John," referring of course, to the privy.

Ice Capades. In 1939, a slip of the tongue by Walter Brown, head of the Boston Garden and the Boston Celtics produced this term. Using a dictionary in an attempt to find a new name for an extravaganza performed on ice, he looked up from the book for a moment and said, "Icecapades," but then immediately corrected himself, saying, "I made a mistake, it's escapades." His partner in this venture, John Harris, said, "No, you didn't. Ice Capades it shall be!"

United States. Thomas Paine, in the second of his Crisis papers, coined the term "United States," which was adopted by the 1777 Articles of Confederation. Boston takes some credit for this event, albeit indirectly. It was a Boston-born Benjamin Franklin who found Thomas Paine working as an apprentice in London. Seemingly fated to a life of obscurity, he was encouraged by Franklin to emigrate to the New World. Finally, Franklin sponsored his way over.

The Smoot. Oliver R. Smoot, M.I.T. class of 1962, was used by his classmates to measure the Massachusetts Avenue bridge (officially, the Harvard Bridge). As a fraternity initiation, his frat brothers kept flipping Smoot end to end and discovered that the bridge is exactly 364 Smoots plus one ear long. When the bridge was rebuilt in 1990, state officials repainted the Smoot measurements first placed there by the students in 1958. Recognized officially by state engineers, the Smoot has been a standard of measure at M.I.T. for over thirty years. (A Smoot, by the way, is exactly sixty-six inches long. The length of his ear, however, is classified information, according to the administration of M.I.T.)

Bloomers. These undergarments were invented by a Boston seamstress, Cornelia Bloomer, in 1851.

Submarine sandwich. The term was first used by a restaurant in Scollay Square at the beginning of World War II to entice the hoards of U.S. Navy personnel stationed at the Charlestown Navy Yard to try this new sandwich. The roll, of course, was baked in the shape of a submarine.

19

The Largest, the Oldest, the Longest, the Shortest, the Fewest, the Greatest and the Best

BOSTON, AMONG ITS many historical treasures, boasts a number of hidden nuggets. See how many of the following you know about.

The Largest

- The largest concentration of colleges and universities in the world is in Boston. Boston has twenty-six four-year colleges and universities in addition to Harvard and M.I.T.

- The Boston Aquarium has the largest cylindrical saltwater tank in the world, holding 187,000 gallons.

- Children's Hospital, founded in 1869, is the largest pediatric medical center in the United States.

- The First Church of Christ Scientist has the largest pipe organ in the western hemisphere. Made by the Aeolian-Skinner organ company, it boasts 13,595 pipes and four keyboards with 200 drawknobs.

- The Head of the Charles Regatta is the largest single day regatta in the world. Over one thousand boats and four thousand rowers compete.

- The largest private library in the world is Widener Library in Harvard Yard. It contains over 12.2 million volumes.

- The largest museum collection of Japanese art and swords outside of Tokyo is in the Boston Museum of Fine Arts.

- The world's largest copyrighted work of art is on the Dorchester gas tank. It was designed by Corita Kent before she withdrew from the Order of the Immaculate Conception. The painting is 150 feet high and covers 73,374 square feet of surface.

- In 1838 the largest hotel in the United States at the time was built at the corner of Lincoln and Beach streets. It was known as the United States Hotel.

- In 1950 the largest robbery in the United States up to that time was the famous Brinks Robbery, which netted over $2.5 million.

- For its time, the largest structure in the world to be used as a free public school was built in 1877, at the corners of Warren, Dartmouth, and Montgomery streets. It then housed the Boston Latin School and Boston English High School. It had a total of sixteen classrooms!

- When completed in 1899, South Station was the largest railroad terminal in the world.

- The largest warehouse in the world was at the old army post in South Boston, now called The Design Center. Rebuilt in 1919, it has over 1.5 million square feet of space. (It was ultimately surpassed by a Russian warehouse built after World War II.)

- The largest teddy bear in the world sits on Boylston Street in front of F.A.O. Schwartz, the children's store. The statue is twelve feet high, weighs two tons, and cost $500,000!

The Oldest

- The oldest marathoner in the world is John Kelley "the elder," who in 1992 ran in his sixty-first Boston Marathon at the age of 84. (Kelley had won this event twice—first in

---

What They Never Told You About Boston

1935 and again in 1945.) After the race, "the elder" announced that he had run his final marathon. Another John Kelley, "the younger," not related to the former, also won this event—in 1957.

- The oldest player to win a major league batting title was Ted Williams, who was forty years old when he won it in 1958 with the Boston Red Sox.

- The oldest concrete outdoor stadium in the United States is Harvard Stadium, completed in 1903. It was built originally as an oval to resemble the Colosseum in Rome.

- The oldest indoor ice arena in the world is the old Boston Arena on St. Botolph Street, built in 1910. It is now owned by Northeastern University and has been renamed the Matthews Arena.

- The oldest professional sports facility is Fenway Park, built in 1912. (It also has the smallest seating capacity, at 34,171.)

- The oldest wooden building in downtown Boston is the Paul Revere House, built circa 1680. However, the oldest in the entire city of Boston is the Blake House, near Edward Everett Square in Dorchester, which dates from 1648.

- The oldest brick building is the Old Corner Book Store on the corner of School and Washington streets, built in 1712.

- The Brattle Bookstore is the successor to America's oldest antiquarian bookstore in continuous operation. It dates back to 1825.

- The oldest church in Boston is the Old North Church, built in 1723.

- The oldest Victory Garden in the United States is in the Fenway District.

- Boston Garden is the oldest indoor professional sports facility in the United States, built in 1928.

- The first and oldest telephone, as well as the first telephone exchange, is exhibited in the Telephone Building at 185

The Largest, the Oldest, the Longest, the Shortest...

Franklin Street. (See Chapter 20, Inventors and Inventions.)

- The oldest continuously operating tavern in the United States is the Warren Tavern in Charlestown, established in 1780.

- The oldest continuously operating restaurant in the United States is the Union Oyster House, serving since 1826.

- The oldest continuously operating hotel in the United States is the Parker House on School Street, founded in 1854.

- The oldest electric beer pump in the United States has been located at Amrhein's on Broadway in South Boston since 1905.

- The oldest commissioned warship in the world is the USS *Constitution*, "Old Ironsides." Permanently berthed at the Charlestown Navy Yard, Old Ironsides was built in the North End in 1798.

The Longest

- The Boston stage production of *Shear Madness* is the longest running non-musical play in the history of the United States. (Starting its twelfh year in 1993, the production had logged over five thousand performances.)

- The longest continuous public green space in urban America is Frederick Law Olmsted's Emerald Necklace, which stretches for seven miles.

- The longest term of service of any Boston mayor was Kevin H. White, at sixteen consecutive years. Mayor White served from 1967 through 1983.

The Shortest

- The shortest suspension bridge in the world is the footbridge that crosses the Swanboat lagoon in the Public Garden.

The Fewest

- Boston, in its 360-plus-year history, has had only four town or city hall sites. And all four of these sites are still in public use. The first town hall, built in 1657, was on the site of what is now the Old State House. When the original building was burned down, the Old State House was built in its place in 1713. This first State House originally doubled as Boston's town hall. Faneuil Hall also served as a city hall for a time. The third site is on School Street. Now called the Old City Hall, this building was erected in 1865 to replace a Bulfinch city hall. The fourth and present City Hall stands in the middle of Government Center.

The Greatest

- The greatest upset in sports history was when the Boston Braves defeated the Philadelphia As in four straight games to win the 1914 World Series. (No Boston team has won the World Series since the Boston Red Sox won in 1918.)

- As of 1992, the greatest number of National Basketball Association world championships (sixteen) is held by the Boston Celtics.

- Also as of 1992, the greatest number of Basketball All-Star appearances by two players from the same team is thirteen; this record is shared by Bob Cousey and John Havlicek, and all of their appearances were as Boston Celtics.

The Best

- The Cafe Budapest won the Best of the Best Dining Award in 1992, making it the best Hungarian Restaurant in the United States.

- Samuel Adams Beer has, since its inception in 1985, won more awards than any other American beer, making it the best beer in America. Moreover, it is the only American beer to both pass Germany's strict beer purity law and so to be imported and served in Germany.

The Largest, the Oldest, the Longest, the Shortest. . .

20

Inventors and Inventions

AS WE SHALL SEE in the following chapter, Bostonians have every reason to be proud of their home-grown patriots, educators, entrepreneurs, theologians, artists, scientists, and others. Boston also boasts some pretty important inventors, as well.

- Alexander Graham Bell invented the telephone in 1875, in a building at the head of Sudbury Street, overlooking Old Scollay Square.

- Samuel F.B. Morse, inventor of the telegraph in 1834, lived in Old Scollay Square.

- Bostonian Albert Champion invented the spark plug in 1915.

- Charles Goodyear actually invented the "vulcanization" process for automobile tires in Roxbury in 1844, although he later applied for the patent out of Woburn, Massachusetts.

- "King" Gillette invented the safety razor in 1901. The Gillette World Shaving Headquarters is still in South Boston.

- The Parker House Hotel invented Parker House rolls and

*Court and Tremont streets from Scollay Square in the
1860s. Here the telephone was invented.*
Courtesy of the Boston Public Library Print Department.

Boston Cream Pie around the turn of the twentieth century.

- Edwin H. Land invented Polaroid film in his home basement laboratory in Cambridge in 1932.

- In 1911, William Filene invented the Automatic Markdown Basement. He also founded the U.S. Chamber of Commerce. Naturally, the first local chamber of commerce in the United States was in Boston.

- As you now have learned, the first computer, the "differential analyzer" was developed at M.I.T. in 1928. The first automatic digital computer was developed at Harvard in 1944.

- The iron lung was invented by Dr. Philip Drinker, a professor at the Harvard School of Public Health, in 1927.

- The pacemaker was invented by Boston Latin School and Harvard graduate, Dr. Paul Zoll, in 1952.

- Artificial skin was invented by Dr. John F. Burke, of Massachusetts General Hospital, and Ioannis V. Yannas, a professor at M.I.T., in 1979.

- The Baldwin apple was developed by Colonel Laommi Baldwin, chief engineer on the Back Bay landfill project in the 1880s.

- The baseball catcher's mask was invented by Frederick Winthrop Thayer, captain of the Harvard University Baseball Club. It was patented in 1878.

21

Boston Born, Boston Educated, or Both

EARLIER IN THIS BOOK you were promised that there would be no more lists. Again you were lied to. The following is a very abbreviated listing of some illustrious Bostonians whom even Bostonians forget are their very own. (Public streets, bridges, squares, halls, schools, towns, or other works named for these individuals are noted in parentheses.)

Theologians

John Eliot
(Square)

William Ellery Channing
(School)

Phillips Brooks
(House—Harvard College)

Edward Everett
(Square)

Mary Baker Eddy

Martin Luther King
(Boulevard)

Philosophers

George Santayana

Henry David Thoreau

William James

Margaret Fuller
(School)

Julia Ward Howe

William Lloyd Garrison
(Street)

Poets and Authors

Amy Lowell
(House for the Elderly)

Henry Wadsworth Longfellow
(Bridge)

Louisa May Alcott
(Street)

Ralph Waldo Emerson
(Place and School)

Henry James

Nathaniel Hawthorne
(Place)

Alice Brown

John Greenleaf Whittier
(Place)

Phyllis Wheatley
(School)

Francis Parkman
(Street and House)

George Ticknor

George V. Higgins

Oliver Wendell Holmes

Harriet Beecher Stowe

Richard Henry Dana

Edwin O'Connor

Artists

John Smibert

Gilbert Stuart
(Street)

John Singer Sargent

John Singleton Copley
(Square)

Leonard Bernstein

Arthur Fiedler
(Footbridge)

Nathaniel Currier

Winslow Homer

Educators

Horace Mann
(School)

Elizabeth Peabody

Francis Child

Lillian Frank Hecht

Pauline Agassiz Shaw
(School)

Mary Peabody Mann

Mother Mary Joseph Rogers

Boston Born, Boston Educated, or Both

Elma Lewis
(School)

John Tileston
(School and Street)

John Silber

Entrepreneurs and Financiers

Samuel and Nathan Appleton
(Street)

James Russell Lowell
(city)

Eben Jordan
(Jordan Marsh department store)

Amos A. Lawrence
(Street and city)

William Filene
(Filene's Basement)

Alfred C. Fuller
(the Brush man)

Thomas Phillips

Ken Olsen

Jack Sidell

Philanthropists

Captain Robert Keayne

Joshua Bates
(School and Library Hall)

Peter Faneuil
(Hall)

Helen Osborne Storrow
(Drive)

Mary Tileston Hemenway
(Street)

Henry Lee Higginson
(School)

An Wang
(The Wang Center for Performing Arts and The Wang
Ambulatory Care Center at Massachusetts General
Hospital)

Benjamin Franklin
(Street)

Isabella Stuart Gardner
(Museum)

Sidney and Norman Rabb

Scientists

Dr. Zabdiel Boylston
(Street)

Percival Lowell

W.T.G. Morton
(Street)

Harold "Doc" Edgerton

Architects

Charles Bulfinch
(Place)

Solomon Willard

H.H. Richardson

Charles F. McKim

I.M. Pei

J.G.F. Bryant

Donald Stuhl

Boston Born, Boston Educated, or Both

Graham Gund

Frederick Law Olmsted
  (Park)

Sculptors

Anne Whitney

Thomas Ball

Richard Greenough
  (Street and Park)

Martin Milmore

Edminia Lewis

Augustus Saint Gaudens

Presidents

John Adams

John Quincy Adams

Theodore Roosevelt

Franklin Delano Roosevelt

John F. Kennedy

All five of these Presidents were educated at Harvard, making Harvard the undisputed "College of Presidents."

22

Two Who
Left Early

THERE WERE TWO very notable individuals who were born in Boston but left very early. Both, coincidentally, left for Boston's "Sister City," the City of Brotherly Love: Philadelphia.

Benjamin Franklin, born at 19 Milk Street in 1706, left Boston in 1723 at the tender age of seventeen. (We learned earlier that anyone who told you that he was born on Franklin Street lied to you!) At the age of ten, Franklin was apprenticed to his brother, James, a printer.

In his autobiography, Ben complained that his brother frequently demeaned him in public and often beat him in private. Although his treatment was no better or no worse than other apprentices received in Boston, Ben thought that he should have been treated as a brother rather than as an apprentice. However, a unique stroke of luck afforded Ben the opportunity to escape from his tyrannical brother.

James Franklin began a newspaper, *The New England Courant*, in 1720. A piece that he subsequently published offended the Assembly and he was imprisoned for a month because he would not divulge the author. When he was released, it was ordered that James Franklin could no longer print the paper called *The New England Courant*. Rather than get around the edict by changing the paper's name, he decided to have it printed under the name of Benjamin Franklin. To avoid censure from having the paper printed by his apprentice, James returned Ben's indenture with full discharge on the back, as evidence of Ben's changed status and fitness. However, Ben was forced to sign new indentures that were to be kept secret. Guessing that his brother would be unlikely to produce the new indentures and expose his ruse, Ben saw an opportunity to leave his brother. When James discovered Ben's intention, he made certain that no other tradesman in Boston would hire him. So Ben then decided to leave. With assistance from a friend, he boarded a ship bound for New York, buying his passage with monies he received from the sale of a few of his books. His friend convinced the ship's captain to board Ben at night and in secret. The concocted story was that Ben had made a mischevious girl pregnant and that the family was forcing him to marry her. On his arrival in New York, Ben offered his services to William Bradford, New York's only printer. Bradford had no work for him but suggested that Ben try his son, who was Philadelphia's only printer and who had recently lost his number-one hand. Benjamin went, was hired, and Boston lost one of her finest sons.

Edgar Allen Poe, born at 62 Carver Street in 1809, left even earlier. He was not even one month old!

A final footnote here on Poe: Historians have always argued as to whether Poe was born somewhere on Hollis Street or on Carver Street. This issue has, apparently been "solved" for future generations as a result of a cab ride by the well-known actor and Poe aficionado, Vincent Price in 1987.

Price had been staying at the Four Seasons Hotel across from the Public Garden and was heading home to California. As Price got into a cab with his wife, the driver immediately recognized his passenger. Remembering that Price gained his early fame acting in movies adapted from Poe stories, and realizing that they were less than five-hundred feet from Carver Street, the cabbie drove right into what is now a dead-end leading from Boylston Street into a cul-de-sac in the bowels of the Transportation Building: the former Carver Street.

"Driver, where are you taking us?" inquired the unflappable Price. "To the birthplace of Edgar Allen Poe, sir," replied the cab driver. Astonished that he had never been told that Poe had been born in Boston, especially since he, Price, had visited the city every summer for over twenty-five years on his way to and from Martha's Vineyard, the actor vowed that he would send a letter expressing his disappointment to the management of his hotel.

"I have visited Poe's gravesite in Philadelphia," mused Price, "and had always assumed that he had been born there. To think that I could have thrown a stone from my hotel window and hit his birthplace, and they never even mentioned it to me!"

It was just a few months after Price arrived home in Los Angeles that the name Carver Street was officially changed to Edgar Allen Poe Way! From that day into the future, that street sign will mark Boston as Poe's birthplace in the minds of all—even though it also may someday be shown to be a lie.

[The cab driver who started this whole Carver Street discussion with Vincent Price just happened to be this very author.]

23

Some Other Important Things They Never Told You

SOME FACTS simply do not fit neatly into categories or within specific chapter titles. As a result, most are lost forever. The following are a miscellany of additional historical facts about Boston that are too good to pass by. Some are fantastic, others grim. And some are just interesting.

- In the second game of a doubleheader on May 20, 1894, Robert "Link" Lowe, playing for the Boston Nationals (later the Braves) became the first player ever to hit four home runs in a single baseball game. Two of the homers came in the third inning.

- John L. Sullivan, the "Boston Strong Boy," was the first American to win the Heavyweight Title of the World, beating Paddy Ryan in 1882.

- Jack Sharkey, the "Boston Gob," who won the world title in 1932 by defeating Max Schmeling in a fifteen-round decision, was the only champ to fight both Jack Dempsey and Joe Louis.

- On January 15, 1919, a fifty-foot-high iron tank containing 2.3 million gallons of molasses exploded in the North End, sending a fifteen-foot tidal wave across Commercial Street to the harbor in the North End. Twenty-one people were drowned in the molasses, forty were injured, and six buildings were swept away into Boston Harbor.

- Nicola Sacco and Bartolomeo Vanzetti were electrocuted for murder on August 23, 1927. One of the most publicized criminal cases in American history, the trial generated international interest due to its socio-political aspects. The execution took place at the Charlestown Prison. Today, this site is the home of Bunker Hill Community College.

- Mayor James Michael Curley, while a prisoner at the Charles Street Jail, ran for Boston's Board of Aldermen and won! Curly, the future governor, congressman, and four-time Mayor, was sentenced to serve ninety days in 1904. (He took the post-office exam for a friend who needed a job.)

- M.I.T., founded in 1861, was first located on Boylston Street in Copley Square, not in Cambridge.

- Although now in Newton, Boston College was founded in Boston in 1863. It was located next to the Church of the Immaculate Conception on Harrison Avenue, near Boston City Hospital. The original building, later to become Boston College High School, still stands.

- Boston, not Chicago, is the windiest major city in the United States, according to the U.S. Weather Service.

- Boston is the ice cream capital of America. Bostonians consume twenty-six gallons of ice cream per capita annually. The consumption is partially a reflection, no doubt, of the tremendous concentration of college students—over 200,000—in the Boston area.

- The Saltonstalls of Boston are the only family in America to have had eleven successive generations graduate from the same college (Harvard).

- Boston's biggest fan was none other than Charles Dickens, who said, "Boston is what I would like the whole United States to be." He also said, "I sincerely believe that the public institutions and charities of Boston are as nearly

The Original Boston College on Harrison Avenue.
From the author's collection.

perfect as the most considerable wisdom, benevolence and humanity can make them."

- Boston's biggest detractor was Edgar Allen Poe, who confessed, "I am heartily ashamed to have been born in Boston." He always referred to the city as "Frogpondium."

- In the South End district on Bristol Street (recently re-named Paul Sullivan Way), between Albany Street and Harrison Avenue, stands a magnificent Florentine Tower. It was built in 1894 as an exact copy of the Palazzo Vecchio in Florence, Italy.

   In the nineteenth century, these Florentine towers were a favorite design for fire stations in the United States. Originally the Bristol Street Fire Station, by 1920 this tower had become the headquarters for the Boston Fire Department. It was used to train firemen in high-rise firefighting techniques such as carrying people down ladders and jumping into hand-held nets. It was also perfect for hanging long fire hoses to dry. In 1961, the Fire Department relocated to Southampton Street, and the building did not have another permanent tenant until 1980, when the City of Boston

The former Bristol Street Fire Station, built in 1894.
From the author's collection.

invited the spaced-starved Pine Street Inn to use the building as a shelter for the homeless.

- When the British put derogatory lyrics to a traditional tune and created the song "Yankee Doodle," carpenter Isaac Sawtell saw a way to diffuse the ridicule: He always whistled this tune on his way to work (building the Highland Street house for the father of Mayor Edwin Curtis in 1775). Thus he proclaimed proudly that he was, indeed, a Yankee Doodle Dandy! Many of his fellow Bostonians followed suit, and Sawtell was henceforth known as Yankee Doodle.

- Finally, I bet they never told you that the name Massachusetts means "Land of the Blue Hills"! To this day, if the atmospheric conditions are just right, the hills in Milton and Braintree (which are called the Blue Hills) appear blue to observers in Boston.

Some Other Important Things They Never Told You

Bibliography

Bacon, Edwin M. *Bacon's Dictionary of Boston.* Boston: Houghton Mifflin, 1886.

Baltzell, E. D. *Puritan Boston and Quaker Philadelphia.* Boston: Beacon Press, 1979.

Bergen, Philip. *Old Boston in Early Photographs.* New York: Dover, 1990.

Berk, Susan, with Bloom, Jill. *Uncommon Boston.* Reading, Mass: Addison-Wesley, 1980.

Bissell, Richard. *You Can Always Tell a Harvard Man.* New York: McGraw Hill, 1962.

Black, Donald C. *Spoonerisms, Sycophants and Sops.* New York: Harper & Row, 1988.

Bunting, Bainbridge. *Houses of Boston's Back Bay.* Cambridge, Mass.: Belknap Press, 1967.

Drake, S.A. *Old Landmarks and Historic Personages of Boston.* Boston: Little Brown, 1900. Reprint. Detroit: Singing Tree Press, 1970.

Fogelson, Robert M. *America's Armories.* Cambridge, Harvard University Press, 1989

Foote, Shelby. *The Civil War.* New York: Vintage Books, 1986.

Funk, C.E. *Thereby Hangs a Tale.* New York: Harper & Brothers, 1950

Hale, Edward Everett. *Historic Boston.* New York: D. Appleton and Co., 1898.

Harris, John. *Historic Walks in Old Boston.* Chester, Ct.: Globe Pequot Press, 1982.

Harris, J.A. *A Statue for America.* New York: Four Winds Press/ Macmillan, 1985.

Holt, A.H. *Phrases and Word Origins.* New York: Dover, 1964.

Homans, J.S. *History of Boston 1630–1856.* Boston: F.C. Moore and Company, 1856.

Labaree, B.W. *The Boston Tea Party.* New York: Oxford University Press, 1964

McIntyre, A.M. *Beacon Hill: A Walking Tour.* Boston: Little Brown, 1975.

Morris, William and Mary. *Dictionary of Word and Phrase Origins.* New York: Harper & Row, 1971.

O'Brien, G.J. *Walks and Talks About Boston.* Boston: Ball Publications, 1916.

O'Connor, Thomas H. *Bibles, Brahmins and Bosses.* Boston: Trustees of the Boston Public Library, 1984.

Ross, M.D. *The Book of Boston: The Victorian Period.* New York: Hastings House Publishers, 1964.

Russell, Pat. *Boston Taxi Flat Rate Guide.* Boston: Boston Police Department, 1990.

Rutman, Davrett B. *Winthrop's Boston.* New York: W.W. Norton, 1965.

Ryan, George. *Botolph of Boston.* Hanover, Mass.: Christopher Publishing House, 1971.

Shackleton, Robert. *The Book of Boston.* Philadelphia: Penn Publishing Company, 1920.

Shelley, H.C. *John Harvard and His Times.* Boston: Little Brown and Company, 1908.

Shenkman, Richard. *I Love Paul Revere, Whether He Rode or Not.* New York: Harper, 1991.

Schofield, W.G. *Freedom by the Bay.* Skokie, Ill.: Rand McNally, 1974.

Stanley, R.W., ed. *Mr. Bulfinch's Boston.* Boston: Old Colony Trust Company, 1963.

Swift, Lindsay. *Literary Landmarks of Boston.* Boston: Houghton Mifflin Company, 1922.

Thwing, Annie H. *The Crooked and Narrow Streets of Boston 1630–1872.* Detroit: Singing Tree Press, 1920.

Veterans' Association of the First Corps of Cadets. Cambridge, Mass.: John L McAdams Industries, 1973

Vexler, R.I. *Massachusetts: Chronology and Documentary Handbook.* Dobbs Ferry, New York: Oceana Publications, 1978.

Weston, G. F., Jr. *Boston Ways.* Boston: Beacon Press, 1957.

Whitehill, Walter Muir. *Boston, A Topographical History.* Cambridge, Mass.: Harvard University Press, 1959.

Boston Statues. Barre, Mass.: Barre Publishers, 1970.

MISCELLANEOUS

Boston Women's Heritage Trail. Boston: Boston Women's Heritage Trail, 1991. (pamphlet)

Index

Boston born and raised, Walt Kelley graduated from the oldest high school in the United States—Boston Latin School—and then graduated from the oldest college—Harvard. He was employed by the oldest (naturally) bank in New England, The First National Bank of Boston; as executive vice president of MetroBank and Trust, and then joined First Security as vice president and controller. After thirteen years in finance, he changed fields and opened a family business which sold sportscards and sports memorabilia. Over the next six years he formed two more companies, one of which failed and caused the other companies to collapse. After this setback, he joined Town Taxi of Boston, where today he drives a cab—he won the "Best Cab Driver in Boston Award" in 1987. He and his wife, Linda, live in Boston.